MW01613922

Peterson's
MASTER
TOEFL
VOCABULARY

PETERSON'S

About Peterson's, A Nelnet Company

Peterson's (www.petersons.com) is a leading provider of education information and advice, with books and online resources focusing on education search, test preparation, and financial aid. Its Web site offers searchable databases and interactive tools for contacting educational institutions, online practice tests and instruction, and planning tools for securing financial aid. Peterson's serves 110 million education consumers annually.

For more information, contact Peterson's, A Nelnet Company, 2000 Lenox Drive, Lawrenceville, NJ 08648; 800-338-3282; or find us on the World Wide Web at: www.petersons.com/about

Portions of this book were previously published in *Reading and Vocabulary Workbook for the TOEFL Exam* and *Ultimate Word Success*.

Editor: Wallie Walker Hammond; Manufacturing Manager: Ray Golaszewski

ISBN-13: 978-0-7689-2328-5

ISBN-10: 0-7689-2328-X

Printed in the United States of America

10 9 8 7 6 5 4 3 2   08 07

First Edition

Petersons.com/publishing

Check out our Web site at www.petersons.com/publishing to see if there is any new information regarding the test and any revisions or corrections to the content of this book. We've made sure the information in this book is accurate and up-to-date; however, the test format or content may have changed since the time of publication.

OTHER TITLES IN SERIES:

Peterson's Master TOEFL Reading

Peterson's Master TOEFL Writing Skills

Contents

Before You Begin

HOW THIS BOOK IS ORGANIZED

If you are preparing for any version of the TOEFL, you are not alone. Almost a million people all over the world took the TOEFL last year. A high score on this test is an essential step in being admitted to undergraduate or graduate programs at almost all colleges and universities in North America. But preparing for this test can be a difficult, often frustrating, experience.

Peterson's Master TOEFL Vocabulary, used as a self-tutor, will help you improve your vocabulary skills. You'll learn many of the "right" words—words you don't already know but that are likely to appear on your test.

- **Top 10 Strategies to Raise Your Score** gives you test-taking strategies.
- **Part I** provides TOEFL vocabulary basics, including strategies for learning and remembering new words.
- **Part II** provides a diagnostic test to determine your strengths and weaknesses.
- **Part III** provides the basic vocabulary review. The words you'll encounter start with those that are relatively simple. They become relatively difficult as you continue through the book. Various learning strategies, such as learning root words, are reviewed.
- **Part IV** consists of two additional practice vocabulary tests. They will show you how well you have mastered the vocabulary skills presented in this book.

SPECIAL STUDY FEATURES

Peterson's Master TOEFL Vocabulary is designed to be user-friendly. To this end, it includes features to make your preparation much more efficient.

Overview

The review chapters begin with a bulleted overview, listing the topics to be covered in the chapter. This will allow you to quickly target the areas in which you are most interested.

Bonus Information

As you work your way through the book, keep your eyes on the margins to find the following:

NOTE

Notes highlight critical information about improving your vocabulary.

TIP

Tips draw your attention to valuable concepts, advice, and shortcuts for tackling the harder vocabulary words.

Summing It Up

The review chapter ends with a point-by-point summary that captures the most important concepts. They are a convenient way to review the chapter's key points.

Practice Tests

The three practice tests, including the diagnostic test, are designed to help you prepare with little anxiety.

YOU'RE WELL ON YOUR WAY TO SUCCESS

The TOEFL tests your vocabulary with "vocabulary-in-context" questions in which you must determine the meaning of words as used in a specific sentence, as well as indirectly through the use of reading comprehension passages and questions. The more words you know, the better your chances of narrowing down the choices to the correct one. *Peterson's Master TOEFL Vocabulary* will help you to fine tune your vocabulary skills.

GIVE US YOUR FEEDBACK

Peterson's publishes a full line of resources to help guide international students through the college admission process.

We welcome any comments or suggestions you may have about this publication and invite you to complete our online survey at www.petersons.com/booksurvey. Or you can fill out the survey at the back of this book, tear it out, and mail it to us at:

> Publishing Department
> Peterson's
> 2000 Lenox Drive
> Lawrenceville, NJ 08648

Your feedback will help us to provide personalized solutions for your educational advancement.

TOP 10 STRATEGIES TO RAISE YOUR SCORE

1. As with other sections of the TOEFL, **be familiar with the directions and examples so you can begin work immediately.**

2. **For each passage, begin by briefly looking over the questions** (but not the answer choices). Try to keep these questions in mind during your reading.

3. **Scan passages to find and highlight the important facts and information.**

4. **Read each passage at a comfortable speed.**

5. **Answer the questions**, referring to the passage when necessary.

6. **Eliminate answers that are clearly wrong** or do not answer the question. If more than one option remains, guess.

7. **Mark difficult or time-consuming answers** so that you can come back to them later if you have time.

8. **Timing is an important factor.** Don't spend more than 10 minutes on any one reading and the questions about it.

9. **Concentration is another important factor.** The reading section is one of the longer sections of the test. Your practice and hard work will help you.

10. **Relax** the night before the exam.

PART I

TOEFL VOCABULARY BASICS

CHAPTER 1   All About TOEFL Vocabulary

All About TOEFL Vocabulary

OVERVIEW

- **Vocabulary on the TOEFL**
- **Strategies for learning and remembering new words**
- **Summing it up**

VOCABULARY ON THE TOEFL

TOEFL vobabulary questions ask you to identify the meanings of words and phrases that appear in the reading passages. The words and phrases that are tested are important to understanding the entire passage, and, for the most part, you will have to figure out their meanings. On the TOEFL iBT, however, if there are technical or unusual words in the passage, you will see the definition presented in a box.

STRATEGIES FOR LEARNING AND REMEMBERING NEW WORDS

Read

Reading is probably the single best way to improve your vocabulary. When you're preparing for the TOEFL, read materials that contain the words that you are most likely to encounter.

Use a Dictionary and Thesaurus

If you're serious about improving your testworthy vocabulary, you must have (and use!) a good dictionary. (A good thesaurus also helps a lot, but more on that later.) A *dictionary* is an alphabetical reference list of the words in the language.

A dictionary entry always includes the following components:

- Spelling
- Pronunciation
- Part(s) of speech
- Irregular forms of the word
- Definition
- Etymology (the derivation and development of words)

An entry may also contain synonyms and antonyms of the word; prefixes, suffixes, and other elements in word formation; and abbreviations.

Most people think that all dictionaries are the same. After all, all dictionaries are chock full of words listed in alphabetical order. They all have pronunciation guides, word definitions, and word histories. However, all dictionaries are *not* the same. Different types of dictionaries fit different needs.

For example, dictionaries have been written just for scholars who research the history of language. The most famous scholarly dictionary is *The Oxford English Dictionary*. An unabridged dictionary, the *OED* (as it's often called) contains more than 500,000 entries. Don't rush right out to buy one to stash in your bookcase, however, because the *OED* now contains about 60 million words in 20 volumes. If shelf space is an issue and you simply can't live without an *OED*, however, online and CD-ROM versions are available from www.oed.com.

Dictionaries have been created just for adults, college students, high school students, and elementary school students, too. The following list includes the bestselling general dictionaries and the Web addresses for the online versions, when available:

- *The American Heritage Dictionary of the English Language* (Houghton Mifflin Co.: www.bartleby.com/61)
- *Merriam-Webster's Collegiate Dictionary* (Merriam-Webster, Inc.: www.m-w.com/dictionary.htm)
- *Merriam-Webster's Pocket Dictionary* (Merriam-Webster, Inc.)
- *The New Shorter Oxford English Dictionary* (Oxford University Press, Inc.)
- *The Random House College Dictionary* (Random House, Inc.)
- *Webster's New World College Dictionary* (Hungry Minds, Inc.)

Which dictionary should you purchase and use? Since more than 30,000 dictionaries are currently offered for sale online, you've got some shopping to do. Here's what you need:

- A dictionary that contains all the words that you are likely to encounter on standardized tests. This will most likely be the same dictionary that you can use in college, in your personal life, and in your professional life.

- The words explained in terms that you can understand.

- A size that fits your needs. You might wish to buy a hardbound dictionary to use at home when you study and a smaller paperback to keep in your backpack or briefcase for immediate reference.

- An online dictionary can't fulfill all your needs, unless you like to tote around your laptop and fire it up all the time. Always have a print dictionary to use, even if you have an online version.

When you're trying to find a word in the dictionary, always begin by making an educated guess as to its spelling. The odds are in your favor. However, the more spelling patterns you know for a sound, the better your chances of finding the word quickly. You can find a pronunciation chart in the beginning of any dictionary. Once you've narrowed down your search and you're flipping through the pages, use the *guide words*, located on the upper-corners of the pages, to guide your search. Then, follow strict alphabetical order.

The following diagram shows how to read a sample entry.

**spelling,
pronunciation**   **part of speech**   **plural**   **definitions**

can-dy (kan'de), *n. pl.* **-dies**, v., **-died, -dying. —n. 1.** any of a variety of confections made with sugar, syrup, etc. combined with other ingredients. **2.** a single piece of such a confection. *—vt:* **3.** to cook in sugar or syrup, as sweet potatoes or carrots. **4.** to cook in heavy syrup until transparent, as fruit, fruit peel, or ginger. **5.** to reduce (sugar, syrup, etc.) to a crystalline form, usually by boiling down. *vi:* to become candied. see vt. [ME *sugre candy* candied sugar < MF *sucre candi*; *candi* << Ar *qandi* or sugar = *qand* sugar (< Pers; perh. orig. piece of sugar candy; if so, akin to Skt khanda piece)]

**etymology
(word history)**

Let's look a little closer at the entry:

- Notice the pronunciation comes right after the entry word. It's in parentheses—(kan'de).

- The part of speech is indicated by the **n.** It's an abbreviation for "noun." Look at the third entry. The *vt:* right before the 3. shows that the word can be used as a transitive verb (a verb that must be followed by a direct object). The *vi:* at the end of the fifth entry shows that the word can also be used as an intransitive verb (a verb that does not need a direct object to make sense in a sentence).

- The *pl.* at the beginning of the entry shows how you can make the word plural (more than one). Here, the singular "candy" becomes the plural "candies."

- The definitions follow the plural forms of the word. The word "candy" has several different meanings. They are arranged by the part of speech: the first definitions show what "candy" means when used as a noun; the second group shows what "candy" means when used as a verb.

- The information at the very end of the entry is the etymology or history of the word. This shows how the word was formed and came into English.

A *thesaurus* is a reference book that contains synonyms and antonyms. The word *thesaurus* comes from a Greek word that means "collection" or "treasure." A thesaurus is especially helpful when you're trying to express an idea but you don't know how to phrase it. It is also a helpful reference book when you are trying to find a better word than the one you've been using. This helps you state exact shades of meaning rather than approximations. As a result, your vocabulary increases by heaps and heaps of words. This is clearly a big advantage when it comes to preparing for a standardized test.

In a thesaurus, words with similar meanings are grouped together. To find a synonym for a word in a traditional print thesaurus, you must use the index at the back of the book. However, new editions and online versions of a thesaurus are arranged like a dictionary in alphabetical order.

If you look up the word *exciting* in a print thesaurus, you would find this entry:

> **excitement** [*n*] *enthusiasm*; *incitement*
> action, activity, ado, adventure, agitation, animation, bother, buzz*, commotion, confusion, discomposure, disturbance, dither*, drama, elation, emotion, excitation, feeling, ferment, fever, flurry, frenzy, furor, fuss, heat*, hubbub*, hullabaloo, hurry, hysteria, impulse, instigation, intoxication, kicks*, melodrama, motivation, motive, movement, passion, perturbation, provocation, rage, stimulation, stimulus, stir, thrill, titillation, to-do, trepidation, tumult, turmoil, urge, warmth, wildness. SEE CONCEPTS 38, 410, 633.

SEE CONCEPTS in the print thesaurus takes you to the *Concept Index*, which helps you link different related ideas. In this way, you can find the exact shade of meaning you need. Use the key in the beginning of the print thesaurus to understand different symbols. In this entry, for example, the * shows that a word is colloquial or the slang level of usage.

Online thesaurus programs are especially useful for distinguishing among homonyms. If you intended to type "*whether*" but instead keyboarded "*weather*," the thesaurus will give you synonyms like *atmospheric conditions*, *climate*, *meteorology*, and *the elements*. This can help you keep your homonyms straight.

While both a print and an online thesaurus unquestionably will help you beef up your vocabulary, in general, a print thesaurus will give you more options than an online thesaurus. That's because the print versions have more words in them. Therefore, you'll need a print thesaurus even if you have an online version. Use a print thesaurus when you need a wider variety of choices.

Pronounce Words Correctly

Knowing the meaning of a word is only half the battle; you also have to know how to pronounce it. It's astonishing how many words are misunderstood simply because they are mispronounced. Words get mangled in surprisingly inventive ways. For example, people often switch letters. For example, *abhor* (hate) becomes uh-*bor* rather than ab-*hor*.

People have also been known to drop letters. For instance, the food poisoning known as *salmonella* is correctly pronounced *sal*-muh-*nel*-uh. Dropping the *L* results in *sam*-uh-nel-uh.

The pronunciation problem is especially acute with words that can function as more than one part of speech. The word *ally* is a case in point. As a noun, it's pronounced *al*-eye. As a verb, it's pronounced uh-*lie*.

In addition, people often insert an extra letter or two, which can make the word unrecognizable. For instance, *ambidextrous* (able to use either hand) has four syllables and is correctly pronounced *am*-bi-*deks*-trus. But sometimes speakers add an extra syllable to get *am*-bi-*deks*-tree-us or *am*-bi-*deks*-tru-us.

Even the lowly word *picture* can get warped as *pitcher*. As a result, no one knows what anyone else is talking about. Incorrect pronunciations can make it impossible to define the word, too.

The most effective way to learn how to pronounce new words is by using a dictionary. Get a reliable desk or pocket dictionary. It's the best source for the words you need to get you where you want to go.

How well do you pronounce testworthy words? Take the following self-test to see. Cover the third column with a piece of paper. Then read each word and its definition. Pronounce each word. Last, check the third column to see how well you did.

Word	Meaning	Pronunciation
Amish	Pennsylvania Dutch	*ah*-mish
aplomb	assurance	uh-*plahm*
awry	wrong, crooked	uh-*ry*
banquet	feast	*bang*-kwit
buffet	self-service meal	buh-*fay*
buoy	floating marker	*boo*-ee
Celtic	Irish	*kel*-tik
denouement	conclusion	*day*-noo-*mah*
entrepreneur	business person	*ahn*-truh-pruh-*nur*
fracas	noisy fight	*fray*-kis
hegemony	leadership	hi-*jem*-uh-nee
insouciant	carefree	in-*soo*-see-int
khaki	light brown	*kak*-ee
larynx	voice box	*lar*-ingks
mausoleum	tomb	*maw*-suh-*lee*-um
niche	corner	*nich* (rhymes with "itch")
penchant	inclination	*pen*-chint
posthumous	after death	*pahs*-chuu-mus
quagmire	swamp	*kwag*-myr
remuneration	payment	ri-*myoo*-nuh-*ray*-shin
shallot	onion	*shal*-it or shuh-*laht*
toupee	hairpiece	too-*pay*
vehement	fiery, passionate	*vee*-uh-mint
verbiage	wordy	*vur*-bee-ij
worsted	yarn	*wuus*-tid

Use Word Cards

One of the most effective ways to make a word your own is through repetition. Going over the word can help you master its meaning as well as pronunciation and usage. Try this idea: buy a stack of 3 × 5 index cards.

As you read through the following chapters, write each difficult word on the front of an index card, one word per card. Then, write the definition on the back. Here's a sample:

FRONT:

matriarch

BACK:

the female head of
a family or tribe

Learn Synonyms and Antonyms

Synonyms are words that are nearly the same in meaning as other words. *Antonyms* are words that are opposites. Learning different synonyms and antonyms can help you swell your vocabulary. Go ahead and try it now.

Complete the following chart by writing at least one synonym and antonym for each word. Then, see how many more synonyms and antonyms you can brainstorm. Possible answers follow.

Word	Synonym	Antonym
1. adapt	_____	_____
2. authentic	_____	_____
3. chronic	_____	_____
4. conquer	_____	_____
5. frustrate	_____	_____
6. indulge	_____	_____
7. naïve	_____	_____
8. punish	_____	_____
9. relinquish	_____	_____
10. sullen	_____	_____

Suggested answers:

Word	Synonyms	Antonyms
1. adapt	adjust, accustom, accommodate	disarrange, dislocate
2. authentic	genuine, real, legitimate	fake, counterfeit, bogus, imitation
3. chronic	habitual, ongoing, constant	one time, single
4. conquer	defeat, vanquish, overwhelm	surrender, yield, forfeit, give up
5. frustrate	baffle, beat, disappoint	facilitate, encourage
6. indulge	tolerate, humor, allow, permit	prohibit, deter, restrain, enjoin
7. naïve	innocent, ingenuous	worldly, urbane, suave
8. punish	discipline, castigate	reward, compensate, remunerate
9. relinquish	quit, renounce	perpetuate, keep
10. sullen	irritable, morose, moody	cheerful, jolly, blithe, happy

Understand a Word's Unstated Meanings

Every word has a *denotation*, its dictionary meaning. In addition, some words have *connotations*, their understood meanings or emotional overtones. For example, both *house* and *home* have the same denotation, a shelter. *Home*, however, carries a connotation of warmtl!and love not present in *house*.

Use Word Parts

A surprisingly large number of words can be divided into parts that you can figure out easily. If you can define the parts, then you can often decode the entire word. This is a crucial skill on standardized tests, when you're under time constraints.

There are three main word parts to know: *roots*, *prefixes*, and *suffixes*.

- A *root* is a base or stem form of many words. Roots are covered in depth in Chapter 5.
- A *prefix* is a letter or a group of letters placed at the beginning of a word to change its meaning. Prefixes are covered in depth in Chapter 6.
- A *suffix* is a letter or a group of letters placed at the end of a word to change its meaning. Suffixes are covered in depth in Chapter 7.

For example, if you know the Latin root *ami* means "like" or "love," you can easily figure out that *amiable* means "pleasant and friendly." Similarly, you could deduce that *amorous* means "loving." Even if you can't define a word exactly, recognizing the different parts of the word still will give you a general idea of the word's meaning.

Use Mnemonics

Mnemonics are memory tricks that help you remember everything from the order of the planets to your grocery list. Mnemonics are another technique you can use to help you distinguish between easily confused words. For example, to remember that *principal* means "main" (as in the principal of a school), look at the last three letters: the *principal* is your pal. To remember that *principle* means "rule," remember that both words end in *le*.

Likewise, *stationary* means "standing still" (both words *stationary* and *standing* contain an "a") while *stationery* is paper used for writing letters (both words *stationery* and *letter* contain "er"). *Desert* and *dessert* become easier to define when you remember that *dessert* has a double "s," like *strawberry shortcake*.

Create your own mnemonics to help you remember the easily confused words that you are most likely to encounter on standardized tests.

Use Context Clues

When you take standardized tests, you'll be expected to define unfamiliar words. You can often get clues to the meaning of unfamiliar words by the information surrounding the word, its *context*. When you use *context* and *context clues*, you interpret a word's specific meaning by examining its relationship to other words in the sentence. To figure out the meaning of the unfamiliar word, you make inferences based on what you already know and the details that you are given in the sentence or paragraph. Here's an example:

> Just after midnight on April 15, 1912, one of the most dramatic and famous of all <u>maritime</u> disasters occurred, the sinking of the *Titanic*. The *Titanic* was the most luxurious ship afloat at the time, with its beautifully decorated staterooms, glittering crystal chandeliers, and elaborate food service.

How can you figure out that *maritime* must mean "related to the sea, nautical"? Use context clues:

What you already know	The *Titanic* was an oceanliner.
Sentence details	"The *Titanic* was the most luxurious ship afloat. . ."

Try it yourself by defining *futile* as it is used in the following passage:

> The "unsinkable" *Titanic* vanished under the water at 2:20 a.m., April 15. There were about 2,200 passengers aboard, and all but about 700 died. The tragedy was made even worse by the crew's <u>futile</u> rescue attempts. Since there were not enough lifeboats, hundreds of people died who could have survived.

Context clues come in different forms. The most common types of context clues include:

- Restatement context clues
- Inferential context clues
- Contrast context clues

Let's look at each type.

Restatement Context Clues

Here's how one writer defined the word *levee* right in the passage:

> The Army Corps of Engineers distributed 26 million plastic bags throughout the region. Volunteers filled each bag with 35 pounds of sand and then stacked them to create *levees*, makeshift barriers against the floodwaters.

Right after the word *levee*, readers get the definition: "makeshift barriers against the floodwaters."

You can also use an entire passage to get a general sense of difficult words. For example, define *epidemic* as it is used in the following sentence: "Nearly 40 million Americans are overweight; obesity has become an *epidemic*." Since the sentence describes the epidemic as affecting "40 million people," odds are good that *epidemic* means "something that happens to a large group of people." Sometimes you won't be able to pinpoint the precise meaning. Here, for instance, you might infer that an *epidemic* indicates a widespread threat, but you might miss the subtle connection between epidemic and disease. Nonetheless, this clue might be just enough to help you define a new word that you encounter on a standardized test.

Each of the following sentences contains a restatement context clue. The unfamiliar word is in *italics* and the definition is in parentheses. As you read, cover the answer in parentheses and see if you can figure it out.

1. Fatty deposits on artery walls combine with calcium compounds to cause *arteriosclerosis*, hardening of the arteries.

    Arteriosclerosis means ("hardening of the arteries")

2. The upper part of the heart on the left side, the left *atrium*, receives blood returning from circulation.

    Atrium means ("the upper part of the heart")

3. In many Native American tribes, the *shaman*, or medicine man, acted as a ceremonial priest.

    Shaman means ("medicine man")

4. I believe that life is short, so we should enjoy what we eat. As a result, I consume mass quantities of *confectioneries*, candies, and keep my dentist on retainer.

    Confectioneries means ("candies")

5. She jumped into the *fray* and enjoyed every minute of the fight.

    Fray means ("fight")

6. As with all electric *currents* or discharges, lightning will follow the *path of least resistance*. This means that it will take the route that is easiest for it to travel on.

    Current means ("discharges")

    the path of least resistance means ("the route that is easiest for it to travel on")

7. Many settlers on the vast American plains in the late nineteenth century used *sod*, or earth, as a building material for their houses.

   > *Sod* means ("earth")

8. Then, arrange a handful of *mulch*, dead leaves, on the top of the soil.

   > *Mulch* means ("dead leaves")

9. Born in 1831, John Styth Pemberton was a *pharmacist*, someone who dispenses medical drugs, who moved to Atlanta, Georgia, in 1869.

   > *Pharmacist* means ("someone who dispenses medical drugs")

10. To make a living, he created so-called *patent medicines*, homemade medicines that were sold without a prescription.

    > *Patent medicines* means ("homemade medicines that were sold without a prescription")

Inferential Context Clues

As you have just read, sometimes the unfamiliar word may be defined right in the text. Other times, however, you will have to *infer* the meaning from what you already know and from details you heard or read. This takes a bit of detective work.

When you *make an inference*, you combine what you already know with spoken or textual clues to discover the unstated information. You may have heard this referred to as "reading between the lines" or "putting two and two together." In graphical form, the process of making an inference looks like this:

Text Clues + What I Know = Inference

Try the following example:

> In 1862, in order to support the Civil War effort, Congress enacted the nation's first income tax law. It was a <u>forerunner</u> of our modern income tax in that it was based on the principles of graduated, or progressive, taxation and of withholding income at the source.

Context Clue	+	What I Know	=	Inference
was a *forerunner*	+	*fore* means "before" or "precede"	=	forerunner means "before"

Contrast Context Clues

You can also figure out an unknown word when an opposite or contrast is presented. When you do this, you're making an inference. For example, you can define *literal* by finding its contrast in the sentence:

> It is hard to use *literal* language when talking about nature because people tend to talk about nature using figurative language.

Literal language must be the opposite of "figurative language". If you know that figurative language is words and expressions not meant to be taken at face value, you can infer that "literal" must mean the *strict or exact meaning*. Other synonyms would include *verbatim* or *word-for-word*.

Use contrast clues to infer the meaning of *menace* in the following sentence:

> I was afraid that my latest mother-in-law would be a *menace* to our already cranky family, but she turned out to be a great peacemaker.

Menace means "threat." You can infer this from the contrast between "menace" and "peacemaker."

The following words express contrast. Watch for them as you read passages on standardized tests.

Expressions That Show Contrast

but	conversely	however	in contrast
on the other hand	still	nevertheless	yet

Using context is an important way to define unfamiliar words on the TOEFL. Use all the different types of context clues as you decode these unfamiliar words in italics.

> Most natural hazards can be detected before their threat matures. But *seisms* (from the Greek *seismos*, earthquake) have no known *precursors*, so they come without warning, like the *vengeance* of an ancient warrior. For this reason, they continue to kill in some areas at a level usually reserved for wars and epidemics—11,000 people in northeastern Iran died on August 31, 1968, not in the ancient past. Nor is the horror of the *lethal* earthquake completed with the heavy death toll. The homeless still living are left to cope with fire, looting, *pestilence*, fear, and the burden of rebuilding what the planet so easily shrugs away.

Word	Pronunciation	Definition
seisms	*si*-zums	earthquakes
precursors	*pre*-cuhr-zurs	warnings, forerunners
vengeance	*ven*-gehnce	revenge, retribution
lethal	*lee*-thal	deadly
pestilence	*pes*-til-ence	a deadly widespread disease, like the plague

The film industry *metamorphosed* from silent films to the "talkies" in the late 1920s, after the success in 1927 of *The Jazz Singer*. Mickey Mouse was one of the few "stars" who made a smooth transition from silent films to talkies with his 1928 cartoon *Steamboat Willie*. Within a year, hundreds of Mickey Mouse clubs had sprung up all across the United States. By 1931, more than a million people belonged to a Mickey Mouse club. The *phenomenon* was not confined to America. In London, Madame Tussaud's *illustrious* wax museum placed a wax figure of Mickey alongside its statues of other *eminent* film stars. In 1933, according to Disney Studios, Mickey received 800,000 fan letters—an average of more than 2,000 letters a day. To date, no "star" has ever received as much fan mail as Mickey Mouse.

Word	Pronunciation	Definition
metamorphosed	meh-tah-*mor*-fozd	changed
transition	tran-*si*-shun	development or change
phenomenon	fe-*nahm*-ih-nan	event, occurrence
illustrious	ih-*lus*-tree-us	distinguished, celebrated
eminent	*eh*-min-ent	famous

A worldwide *economic* Depression in the 1930s left many people unemployed. One such person was Charles Darrow of Philadelphia, Pennsylvania, who had lost his job as a heating engineer. To try to make a living, Darrow invented a board game he called "Monopoly." *Initially*, Darrow tried to sell his idea to the leading game manufacturer in America, but Parker Brothers turned the game down because it felt the game was too *elaborate* to play. In *desperation*, Darrow used his own money to have 5,000 games made by a small company. He sold the games himself, and the *craze* spread. Seeing the success of the game, Parker Brothers changed its mind and purchased the game for manufacturing and distribution. In 1975, twice as much Monopoly money was printed in the United States as real money. All told, nearly 100 million Monopoly sets have been sold since 1935.

Word	Pronunciation	Definition
economic	eek-a-*nom*-ik	having to do with money
initially	in-*ih*-shall-ee	at first
elaborate	i-*lab*-or-it	complex
desperation	des-per-*a*-shun	extreme need
craze	*crayz*	fad, fashion

Context clues are especially crucial when you encounter words with more than one meaning. The word *favor*, for example, has many different meanings. Here are six of them: *a kind act, friendly regard, being approved, a gift, to support,* and *to resemble*.

When you read, you often come across a word that you think you know but that doesn't make sense in the sentence you're reading. That's your clue that the word has more than one meaning. In this case, you must choose the meaning that fits the context.

Follow these three simple steps:

1. Read the sentence and find the word with multiple meanings.
2. Look for context clues that tell you which meaning fits.
3. Substitute a synonym for the word and see if it makes sense. If not, try another meaning for the word. Continue until you find the right meaning.

For example: Nico was <u>resigned</u> to working overtime on Friday night.

1. *Resigned* has multiple meanings. *Resigned* means "quitting a job." It also means "giving in unhappily but without resistance.'
2. Since Nico is working overtime, he is not quitting his job. Therefore, the second meaning of *resigned* should fit.
3. Using the synonym *agreeable* for *resigned*: Nico was <u>agreeable</u> to working overtime on Friday night. The sentence makes sense, so you have found the correct meaning for *resigned*.

Here are some examples of multiple-meaning words:

Word	Example	Meaning	Example	Meaning
address	home <u>address</u>	residence	graduation <u>address</u>	speech
game	play a <u>game</u>	sport	have a <u>game</u> leg	injured
catholic	<u>catholic</u> tastes	universal, wide	<u>Catholic</u> religion	of the Roman church
rash	have a <u>rash</u>	skin problem	<u>rash</u> action	hasty

Learn Word Histories

In the 1600s, people believed that toads were poisonous, and anyone who mistakenly ate a toad's leg instead of a frog's leg would die. Rather than swearing off frog's legs, people sought a cure for the "fatal" food poisoning. Performing in public, "quack" healers would sometimes hire an accomplice who would pretend to eat a toad, at which point his employer would whip out an instant remedy and "save" his helper's life. For his duties, the helper came to be called a "toad-eater." Since anyone who would consume anything as disgusting as a live toad must be completely under his master's thumb, "toad-eater" or "toady" became the term for a bootlicking, fawning flatterer.

And that's how the word *toady* came to be. English is a living language. From its Germanic beginnings, English absorbed influences from a wide variety of sources, including classical Greek and Latin to Italian, French, Spanish, and Arabic languages. English continues to absorb new words as our culture changes. In addition, a significant part of our vocabulary is artificially created to meet new situations. Exploring the history of these words, their *etymology*, can help you learn many useful everyday words.

Vocalize as You Learn

Saying words aloud or hearing somebody else say them helps you to recall them later. Try reading sample sentences and definitions aloud as well.

Review, Review, Review

It's not enough to "learn" a word once. Unless you review it, the word will soon vanish from your memory banks. This book is packed with quizzes and word games to help refresh your memory.

SUMMING IT UP

- Vocabulary questions on the TOEFL ask you to identify the meanings of words and phrases as they appear in the reading passages.

- The strategies for learning and remembering new words are:

    Read.

    Use a dictionary or thesaurus.

    Pronounce words correctly.

    Use word cards.

    Learn synonyms and antonyms.

    Understand a word's unstated meanings.

    Use word parts.

    Use mnemonics.

    Use context clues.

    Learn word histories.

    Vocalize as you learn.

    Review, review, review.

PART II

DIAGNOSING STRENGTHS AND WEAKNESSES

CHAPTER 2   Practice Test 1: Diagnostic

ANSWER SHEET PRACTICE TEST 1: DIAGNOSTIC

1. Ⓐ Ⓑ Ⓒ Ⓓ   6. Ⓐ Ⓑ Ⓒ Ⓓ   11. Ⓐ Ⓑ Ⓒ Ⓓ
2. Ⓐ Ⓑ Ⓒ Ⓓ   7. Ⓐ Ⓑ Ⓒ Ⓓ   12. Ⓐ Ⓑ Ⓒ Ⓓ
3. Ⓐ Ⓑ Ⓒ Ⓓ   8. Ⓐ Ⓑ Ⓒ Ⓓ   13. Ⓐ Ⓑ Ⓒ Ⓓ
4. Ⓐ Ⓑ Ⓒ Ⓓ   9. Ⓐ Ⓑ Ⓒ Ⓓ   14. Ⓐ Ⓑ Ⓒ Ⓓ
5. Ⓐ Ⓑ Ⓒ Ⓓ   10. Ⓐ Ⓑ Ⓒ Ⓓ   15. Ⓐ Ⓑ Ⓒ Ⓓ

answer sheet

PRACTICE TEST 1: DIAGNOSTIC

> **Directions:** In questions 1–15 each sentence has a word or phrase underlined. Below each sentence there are four other words or phrases, marked (A), (B), (C), and (D). You are to choose the *one* word or phrase that *best keeps the meaning* of the original sentence if it is substituted for the underlined word or phrase.

Q His students think he is odd.

- **(A)** dangerous
- **(B)** friendly
- **(C)** strange
- **(D)** humorous

A **The correct answer is (C).** The sentence, "His students think he is strange," is closest in meaning to, "His students think he is odd."

As soon as you understand the directions, begin work on the problems.

1. Oil is one of the <u>principal</u> sources of energy.
   - **(A)** most expensive
   - **(B)** most important
   - **(C)** most difficult
   - **(D)** most popular

2. No one can <u>survive</u> for very long without water.
   - **(A)** reproduce
   - **(B)** prosper
   - **(C)** transcend
   - **(D)** exist

3. The assignment was to write a <u>synopsis</u> of our favorite novel.
   - **(A)** evaluation
   - **(B)** summary
   - **(C)** critique
   - **(D)** dramatization

4. It is <u>futile</u> to go shopping when you don't have any money.
   - **(A)** useless
   - **(B)** brilliant
   - **(C)** idiotic
   - **(D)** challenging

5. The actress had to raise her voice in order to be <u>audible</u> in the balcony.
   - **(A)** musical
   - **(B)** dramatic
   - **(C)** heard
   - **(D)** appreciated

6. Dictators do not <u>tolerate</u> opposition of any kind.
   - **(A)** understand
   - **(B)** permit
   - **(C)** justify
   - **(D)** execute

7. Earthquakes occur <u>frequently</u> in parts of California.
   - **(A)** instantly
   - **(B)** annually
   - **(C)** spontaneously
   - **(D)** often

8. The Rev. Dr. Martin Luther King fought to put an end to racial <u>segregation</u> in the United States.
   - **(A)** integration
   - **(B)** education
   - **(C)** separation
   - **(D)** torture

9. The number of <u>illiterate</u> young people in her country continues to rise.

    (A) unable to read and write

    (B) without children

    (C) sports participants

    (D) wealthy

10. Since his wound was <u>superficial</u>, only a small bandage was required.

    (A) frivolous

    (B) on the surface

    (C) deep

    (D) supercilious

11. The main road will be closed until the <u>blizzard</u> ends.

    (A) snowstorm

    (B) hurricane

    (C) tornado

    (D) thunderstorm

12. Tennis wear has become a very <u>lucrative</u> business for both manufacturers and tennis stars.

    (A) illegal

    (B) circumstantial

    (C) expansive

    (D) profitable

13. A familiar <u>adage</u> says that the early bird gets the worm.

    (A) proverb

    (B) lady

    (C) gentleman

    (D) book

14. A television ad shows a busy baker with a new computer that the advertiser claims will help him "make <u>dough</u>."

    (A) a baking mixture

    (B) more customers

    (C) money

    (D) bread

15. At every faculty meeting, Ms. Volatile always manages to <u>put her foot in her mouth</u>.

    (A) trip over her big feet

    (B) say the wrong thing

    (C) move rapidly

    (D) fall asleep

ANSWER KEY AND EXPLANATIONS

1.	B	6.	B	11.	A
2.	D	7.	D	12.	D
3.	B	8.	C	13.	A
4.	A	9.	A	14.	C
5.	C	10.	B	15.	B

1. **The correct answer is (B).** If your answer is wrong, write the word on a 3 × 5-inch card. Include the synonyms *main*, *chief*, and *major*. As you continue to study in this book, add to your file all words that you discover you do not know. Keep the cards in alphabetical order for easy reference.

2. **The correct answer is (D).** All four choices can be used to make a meaningful sentence. Therefore, you had to know that *survive* is the same as (D), *exist*. If you do not know the meaning of the words given as alternatives, add them to your card list.

3. **The correct answer is (B).** If you know that *critique* and *evaluation* have approximately the same meaning, *critical writing*, then you can assume that neither is the correct answer. *Dramatization* of a novel would certainly not be an assignment a teacher would give. By elimination and using your good sense, you get the correct answer.

4. **The correct answer is (A).** Neither *brilliant* nor *challenging* would describe the experience of shopping with no money. *Idiotic* is not a word used to describe the shopping experience.

5. **The correct answer is (C).** All of the alternatives relate to an actress's experience on stage. The key word in this sentence is *balcony*. What would be necessary for an actress if there are people in the balcony? She would have to be (C), *heard*, not *musical*, *dramatic*, or *appreciated*.

6. **The correct answer is (B).** The key words in this sentence are *dictators* and *opposition*. You know that dictators by nature do not (B), *permit* opposition, so the other three alternatives will not fit with what you know about dictators.

7. **The correct answer is (D).** The word *frequently* is commonly used, so you should know its meaning.

8. **The correct answer is (C).** Knowing about Martin Luther King will help you answer this item correctly. The fact that *segregation* and *separation* both begin with *se* may lead you to the correct answer here. However, there is no guarantee that all words that begin with the same syllable will mean the same thing.

9. **The correct answer is (A).** The word *illiterate* is composed of two parts—*il*, which is a prefix meaning *not*, and *literate*, which means *able to read and write*.

10. **The correct answer is (B).** The prefix *super* means *above*. Another clue is that only a small bandage is needed, so the wound must not be *deep*. It is true that a *frivolous* person is *superficial*, but the word applies to people not to inanimate things. *Supercilious* might be the correct answer, since it begins with the same prefix. You would have to know that *supercilious* means *haughty* and therefore applies only to people.

11. **The correct answer is (A).** All four alternatives relate to a serious weather disturbance. You would have to know that only a *blizzard* creates the hazard of snow.

12. **The correct answer is (D).**

13. **The correct answer is (A).** Familiarity with old sayings such as the one given in this sentence—the early bird gets the worm—will give you answer (A), *proverb*. The other alternatives are senseless in the context of this sentence.

14. **The correct answer is (C).** This is a difficult item because the word *dough* is a slang expression for (C), *money*. The advertiser is making a play on words to get a humorous effect, since a baker necessarily makes dough, a mixture of flour and water. The computer will help the baker make more money, not more baking mix.

15. **The correct answer is (B).** *To put your foot in your mouth* is an idiomatic expression that means (B), *to say the wrong thing*. Like most such expressions, this would be impossible to translate literally into another language. It has simply become a frequently used expression that is generally understood by native speakers. Another such expression is *to have a heart*, which means *to be sympathetic*.

PART III

TOEFL VOCABULARY REVIEW

Words in Context

OVERVIEW

- **Strategies for defining words from context**
- **Summing it up**

At some point, there may be a word you do not know the meaning of and there may be no prefix or root to help you. In this case, you must look at the context of the word.

The context of a word is the setting in which the word occurs in speech or in written materials. You usually learn words by hearing or seeing them in context, and developing this ability will help you learn more words.

The following includes exercises for words in context. These passages and vocabulary exercises are not as difficult as those you might find on the TOEFL since the purpose of this book is to teach vocabulary.

STRATEGIES FOR DEFINING WORDS FROM CONTEXT

- In some cases, if you come across an unusual word, the definition of the word is close to it. Try to understand the definition and apply it to the word in context.

- Look for another word or phrase in the context that has the same meaning.

- In some contexts, direct clues are not given but are implied. In this case, you must think about the context and guess what the meaning of the word can be. Even if you cannot determine its exact meaning, you will be able to determine its general meaning.

- Every time you read, practice looking for contextual clues. This will encourage you to analyze the meaning of what you read and will also train you to think about words and their meanings.

chapter 3

As you read the following passage, see if you can get the meaning of the underlined words from the context in which they appear. Then, do the vocabulary builders that follow.

To the Editor:

Your article on plans for aiding the <u>elderly</u> to pay their housing costs was not quite clear in several aspects. I would like to clarify the requirements and exemptions available for those who qualify.

In the first place, a <u>tenant</u> 62 years old or older must live in a rent-controlled or rent-stabilized dwelling, pay more than one third of his or her income for rent, and have a yearly income of $8,000 or less. Such a tenant must apply for exemption from rent increases and must reapply each year thereafter. Once is not enough. It is understood, however, that should the landlord make a major improvement, a new <u>furnace</u> for example, all tenants must accept rent raises to pay for increased comfort. The elderly, poor tenant is not <u>excluded</u> from such a rent increase.

Landlords receive tax exemptions as <u>reimbursement</u> for the money they lose in not increasing rent for the elderly. In New York City, the cost of these tax reductions is $41 million a year, a <u>tremendous</u> figure, but likely to be higher if more of the poor elderly learn they may apply for exemptions. The city is so slow in <u>processing</u> applications that some tenants have paid the full rent. They ought not to have done so. They are fully protected by the law and, once they have applied for exemption, they do not have to pay rent increases.

I appeal to you to clarify this issue so that the elderly poor of our city may become <u>aware</u> of the housing benefits for which they <u>qualify</u>.

Clara Torres
Office of Housing for the Elderly

Vocabulary Builder 1

Directions: Choose the correct meaning of the underlined word.

1. Tenants over 62 can apply for benefits at the Office of Housing for the <u>Elderly</u>.

    (A) poor

    (B) people over 62

    (C) people who need aid

    (D) people who need housing

2. If you don't get that <u>furnace</u> repaired before winter, we will freeze to death.

    (A) fire escape

    (B) heater

    (C) water container

    (D) staircase

3. Since landlords get <u>reimbursements</u>, they shouldn't complain about losing money.

   (A) bills

   (B) increases

   (C) payments

   (D) housing benefits

4. The elderly are not <u>excluded</u> from rent raises that all tenants have to pay when the landlord makes a major improvement.

   (A) obliged

   (B) included

   (C) excited

   (D) eliminated

5. When their rent increased from $200 to $400 a month, they protested against such a <u>tremendous</u> increase.

   (A) light

   (B) difficult

   (C) huge

   (D) tiring

6. Because the city is slow in <u>processing</u> applications, many of the elderly do not get housing benefits.

   (A) providing

   (B) working on

   (C) raising

   (D) trying

7. The landlord notified his <u>tenants</u> that their rent would be increased the following month.

   (A) janitors

   (B) friends

   (C) occupants

   (D) poor people

8. Reading a daily newspaper will make you <u>aware</u> of what is going on in the world.

   (A) knowledgeable

   (B) ignorant

   (C) alike

   (D) dependent

Vocabulary Builder 1 Answers

1. The correct answer is (B).

2. The correct answer is (B).

3. The correct answer is (C).

4. The correct answer is (D).

5. The correct answer is (C).

6. The correct answer is (B).

7. The correct answer is (C).

8. The correct answer is (A).

Vocabulary Builder 2

Directions: Try to get the meaning of the underlined word from its context in the following sentences. Choose the correct synonym. If you cannot figure it out, look the word up in your dictionary.

1. It is <u>inevitable</u> that smoking will damage your health.
   (A) invading
   (B) unhealthy
   (C) unavoidable
   (D) intriguing

2. What you need after a hard week's work is a little <u>frivolity</u> over the weekend.
   (A) luxury
   (B) harmony
   (C) fireworks
   (D) triviality

3. The general planned a new <u>stratagem</u> to conquer the rebel forces.
   (A) strafing
   (B) scheme
   (C) bomb
   (D) headquarters

4. Only a <u>quack</u> would recommend a lettuce diet to an athlete.
   (A) charlatan
   (B) duck
   (C) coach
   (D) doctor

5. The expression "out of the frying pan and into the fire" means to go from one <u>dilemma</u> to a worse one.

    (A) situation

    (B) predicament

    (C) embarrassment

    (D) aura

6. He made one last <u>futile</u> effort to convince her and left the house.

    (A) difficult

    (B) favorable

    (C) firm

    (D) ineffectual

7. After climbing to the <u>zenith</u>, he slowly worked his way down the mountain.

    (A) zero

    (B) top

    (C) cabin

    (D) mountain

8. A <u>glib</u> answer will not serve for a serious question.

    (A) gross

    (B) capable

    (C) facile

    (D) ignorant

9. Mary set off on her vacation with the intention of finding a tall, dark, handsome, <u>debonair</u> companion.

    (A) doleful

    (B) decent

    (C) urbane

    (D) mercenary

10. Ponce de Leon searched in vain for a means of <u>rejuvenating</u> the aged.

    (A) making young again

    (B) making weary again

    (C) making wealthy again

    (D) making merry again

Vocabulary Builder 2 Answers

1. The correct answer is (C).
2. The correct answer is (D).
3. The correct answer is (B).
4. The correct answer is (A).
5. The correct answer is (B).
6. The correct answer is (D).
7. The correct answer is (B).
8. The correct answer is (C).
9. The correct answer is (C).
10. The correct answer is (A).

Many English words are made up of a combination of word elements. A *root* is a word element, often taken from Latin or Greek, that serves as a base to which other elements are added to modify the root itself. A *prefix* is a word element placed at the beginning of a root, and a *suffix* is attached to the end of a root or word. Both prefixes and suffixes change the meaning of the root and form a new word.

Recognizing and understanding word elements provide a valuable system of analyzing words, figuring out their meaning, and comparing them to find relationships with words you already know. Using this system, you will also be able to organize and learn words in groups rather than individually.

Here are some common Latin and Greek prefixes. Study them and look up the meanings of the words you do not know in the **Example** column.

Prefix	Meaning	Example
ab, a	away from	abduct, amoral
ad, ac, ag, at	to	advent, accrue, aggressive, attracts
ante	before	antedated
anti	against	antipathy
bene	well	benefit
circum	around	circumnavigate
com, con, col	together	compliant, conducive, collate
contra	against	contrary
de	from, down	delete, descend
dis, di	apart	disperse, dilate
ex, e	out	exit, elicit

Prefix	Meaning	Example
extra	beyond	extracurricular
hyper	excessively	hypertension, hyperactive
in, im, il, ir, un	no	intrepid, impossible, illicit, irreparable, unlikely
inter	between	intercultural
intra, intro, in	within	intramural, introduction, inside
mal	bad	malediction
per	through	permeate
peri	around	perimeter
post	after	postoperative
pre	before	precedence, predecessor
pro	forward, for	propose, proponents
re	again	review
semi	half	semicolon
sub	under	submarine
super	above	supervisor
trans	across	transport

Vocabulary Builder 3

Directions: Use the words in the **Example** column, above, to complete these sentences.

1. The men had to _____ their canoe through the woods to the river's edge.
    carry across

2. That sentence requires a(n) _____.
    half colon

3. His _____ condition was excellent.
    after the operation

4. The law requires that there be a(n) _____ from the second floor apartment.
    way out

5. Magellan _____ the world.
    sailed around

6. Our new president is much more popular than his _____.
    one who came before

7. After the protest march, the crowd _____.
    split apart

8. In the evolution of animals, plants _____ insects.
    came before

9. We never agree; his opinions are always _____ to mine.
    against

10. There seems to be a natural _____ between cats and dogs.
    feeling against

11. Workmen at the refinery find that the smell of oil _____ their clothing.
    goes through

12. Students engage in many _____ activities.
    beyond the curriculum

13. The Greek and Turkish students had a(n) _____ exchange.
    between two cultures

14. It is _____ for him to see you today.
    not possible

15. Living in a(n) _____ is most confining.
    underwater vehicle

16. He got a job as a(n) _____ in a dress manufacturing company.
    person above

17. The chairman of the board takes _____ over the other board members.
    right to come before

18. The _____ of conservation protested against strip-mining.
    people for

19. Cutting your salt consumption will _____ your health.
    do well for

20. The professor has to _____ his test papers.
    put together

21. Let's _____ our algebra for the exam tomorrow.
    go over again

22. The terrorists planned to _____ the American general.
    take away

23. Some students give more of their time to _____ sports than to their
    assignments.   within the school

24. What is the _____ of this triangle?
    distance around

25. A magnet _____ iron and its alloys.
    draws to itself

Vocabulary Builder 3 Answers

1. The correct answer is transport.

2. The correct answer is semicolon.

3. The correct answer is postoperative.

4. The correct answer is exit.

5. The correct answer is circumnavigated.

6. The correct answer is predecessor.

7. The correct answer is dispersed.

8. The correct answer is antedated.

9. The correct answer is contrary.

10. The correct answer is antipathy.

11. The correct answer is permeates.

12. The correct answer is extracurricular.

13. The correct answer is intercultural.

14. The correct answer is impossible.

15. The correct answer is submarine.

16. The correct answer is supervisor.

17. The correct answer is precedence.

18. The correct answer is proponents.

19. The correct answer is benefit.

20. The correct answer is collate.

21. The correct answer is review.

22. The correct answer is abduct.

23. The correct answer is intramural.

24. The correct answer is perimeter.

25. The correct answer is attracts.

Study these suffixes. Be sure that you understand what each of the words in the **Example** column means before you do the exercise.

Suffix	Meaning	Example
able, ible	capable of being	expendable, comprehendible
al	relating to	traditional
ance	relating to	alliance
ary	relating to	aviary
ation	action	provocation
cy	quality	potency
ence	relating to	complacence
er	one who	worker
fy	make	beautify
ic	pertaining to	atmospheric
ious	full of	gracious
ist	person who practices	psychiatrist
ity	condition	complexity
ize	to make like	stabilize
less	without	penniless
ment	result, state	contentment

Vocabulary Builder 4

Directions: From the **Example** column above, choose a word that best fits the following definitions.

1. A person with no money is _____.

2. Something that is potent has _____.

3. The state of being content is called _____.

4. Something capable of being comprehended is _____.

5. A person full of grace is _____.

6. A celebration that has become a tradition is considered _____.

7. Two countries that are allied form a(n) _____.

8. The area where birds (avi) are kept is called a(n) _____.

9. Something capable of being expended is considered _____.

10. When weather forecasters talk about the pressure of the atmosphere, they refer to _____ pressure.

11. A person who practices psychiatry is a(n) _____.

12. Someone who works is a(n) _____.

13. If something is described as complex, we can say it has _____.

14. When someone provokes you, we can say he or she has given you _____.

15. When you make something stable, you _____ it.

16. A complacent person is noted for his or her _____.

17. To make a house beautiful is to _____ it.

Vocabulary Builder 4 Answers

1. **The correct answer is penniless.**

2. **The correct answer is potency.**

3. **The correct answer is contentment.**

4. **The correct answer is comprehendible.**

5. **The correct answer is gracious.**

6. **The correct answer is traditional.**

7. **The correct answer is alliance.**

8. **The correct answer is aviary.**

9. **The correct answer is expendable.**

10. **The correct answer is atmospheric.**

11. **The correct answer is psychiatrist.**

12. **The correct answer is worker.**

13. **The correct answer is complexity.**

14. **The correct answer is provocation.**

15. **The correct answer is stabilize.**

16. **The correct answer is complacence.**

17. **The correct answer is beautify.**

Vocabulary Builder 5

Directions: See if you can use the suffixes given in the previous exercise to form new words. When you have finished, check your dictionary to make sure you spelled all the words correctly.

1. Someone who employs others is a(n) _____.

2. A person who favors conservation is a(n) _____.

3. The condition of being sane is _____.

4. Something giving comfort is _____.

5. Something full of infection is _____.

6. The result of adjusting is _____.

7. A person without sense is _____.

8. A person with ideals is a(n) _____. We can say he or she is _____.

9. A lenient judge is noted for his _____.

10. To commit something to memory is to _____ it.

11. A turbulent sea is characterized by its _____.

12. To excite intensely as if by an electric shock is to _____ another person.

Vocabulary Builder 5 Answers

1. **The correct answer is employer.**

2. **The correct answer is conservationist.**

3. **The correct answer is sanity.**

4. **The correct answer is comfortable.**

5. **The correct answer is infectious.**

6. **The correct answer is adjustment.**

7. **The correct answer is senseless.**

8. **The correct answer is idealist/idealistic.**

9. **The correct answer is leniency.**

10. **The correct answer is memorize.**

11. **The correct answer is turbulence.**

12. **The correct answer is electrify.**

Vocabulary Builder 6

Directions: Here are ten groups of words that are frequently confused and misused. Look at the definitions; then fill in the correct word in the sentences.

1. adapt, adopt

    Adapt means to adjust.

    Adopt means to take by choice.

    (A) The committee decided to _____ the new regulations.

    (B) It is difficult to _____ to a new environment.

2. adverse, averse

    Adverse means acting against.

    Averse means having a strong dislike.

    (A) The jury made an _____ decision, so he was hanged.

    (B) An anorexic is _____ to food.

3. allusion, delusion, illusion

    Allusion means an implied or indirect reference.

    Delusion means a false belief.

    Illusion means an unreal image.

    (A) That poor man is under the _____ that he is the president.

    (B) I am not familiar enough with mythology to understand all the _____ s to it in this poem.

    (C) A good painter can give you the _____ of broad space in his works.

4. complement, compliment

    Complement means to complete or make perfect.

    Compliment means to praise.

    (A) I must _____ you on your choice of flowers for the party.

    (B) They are just the right flowers to _____ the table setting.

5. council, counsel

    Council means an elected group to make decisions.

    Counsel means advice.

    (A) The _____ advised the president to raise taxes.

    (B) The group was famous for its good _____.

6. elicit, illicit

    Elicit means to draw out.

    Illicit means against a law or rule.

    (A) The detective attempted to _____ information about the

    (B) _____ drug ring.

7. explicit, implicit

   Explicit means clear and fully expressed.

   Implicit means meant though not plainly expressed.

   (A) The manual gives _____ instructions on how to repair a bicycle.

   (B) There was definitely an _____ threat in the way he glared at her.

8. ingenious, ingenuous

   Ingenious means clever at inventing things.

   Ingenuous means simple, naive, and inexperienced.

   (A) An _____ high school student invented a video game.

   (B) Katy is so _____ she will believe anything you tell her.

9. infer, imply

   Infer means to draw the meaning from.

   Imply means to suggest.

   (A) I_____ from what you just said that the engagement is over.

   (B) Did you mean to _____ that you don't love me anymore?

10. immigrate, emigrate

    Immigrate means to come into a country to make one's home there.

    Emigrate means to leave one's country to go and live in another.

    (A) Many venturesome people _____ from England to Australia.

    (B) If you _____ to this country, you will have to learn the language.

Vocabulary Builder 6 Answers

1. **A.** adopt

   B. adapt

2. **A.** adverse

   B. averse

3. **A.** delusion

   B. allusion

   C. illusion

4. **A.** compliment

   B. complement

5. **A.** council

   B. counsel

6. **A.** elicit

   B. illicit

7. **A.** explicit

   B. implicit

8. **A.** ingenious

   B. ingenuous

9. **A.** infer

   B. imply

10. **A.** emigrate

    B. immigrate

Vocabulary Builder 7

Directions: Write the word next to the definition. Your answers are words used in this chapter.

1. A one-room apartment _____

2. Occupant of a building _____

3. Advanced in years _____

4. Repayment _____

5. Machine for heating a building _____

6. Hint _____

7. A clever trick to obtain an end _____

Vocabulary Builder 7 Answers

1. **The correct answer is studio.**

2. **The correct answer is tenant.**

3. **The correct answer is elderly.**

4. **The correct answer is reimbursement.**

5. **The correct answer is furnace.**

6. **The correct answer is imply.**

7. **The correct answer is stratagem.**

When a word has more than one meaning, the dictionary will number each separate definition; the first meaning given is usually the most common use of the word. When looking up a word in the dictionary, you should know which definition provides the meaning of the word as it is used in the particular context.

Vocabulary Builder 8

Directions: Choose the appropriate definitions for the underlined words. Write the number in the space provided.

1. **(1)** on the surface; not deep

   (2) not serious; not complete

   _____ The article gave a <u>superficial</u> analysis of the country's economic woes.

   _____ The parachutist was treated for <u>superficial</u> cuts and bruises.

2. **(1)** working very well; sharp

   (2) severe; strong

   _____ She suffered from <u>acute</u> back pain after the accident.

   _____ Most animals have an <u>acute</u> sense of smell.

3. **(1)** thoroughly planned

   (2) intentional; on purpose

   _____ It was an accident; she didn't break the vase <u>deliberately</u>.

   _____ The President is taking <u>deliberate</u> steps to balance the federal budget.

4. **(1)** merciful in judgment

   (2) allowing less than the highest standards

   _____ Some people felt that the jury was too <u>lenient</u> with the man who shot the senator.

   _____ It is believed that <u>lenient</u> teachers produce mediocre students.

5. **(1)** concerning people who have a close relationship

   (2) personal; private

   _____ The two women are <u>intimate</u> friends.

   _____ They share even their most <u>intimate</u> thoughts.

6. **(1)** to become or make strong

   (2) to combine into fewer or one

   _____ The two major labor unions <u>consolidated</u> to form one large powerful union.

   _____ The United States is attempting to <u>consolidate</u> its position in the Caribbean.

7. **(1)** to eat or drink

    (2) to use up

    (3) to destroy

    _____ The entire apartment was <u>consumed</u> by fire.

    _____ The tennis player contracted hepatitis after <u>consuming</u> tainted fish.

    _____ Typing his boss's correspondence <u>consumed</u> most of the secretary's time.

8. **(1)** a particular government

    (2) a plan to improve one's health

    _____ After following a strict <u>regime</u>, the injured gymnast returned to competition.

    _____ The nation is sure to prosper under the new <u>regime</u>.

9. **(1)** causing a feeling of pity

    (2) worthless; unsuccessful

    _____ The supervisor is so <u>pathetic</u> that his entire staff is threatening to resign.

    _____ We were awakened by the kitten's <u>pathetic</u> cries.

10. **(1)** to cause to have no effect

    (2) to disprove; deny

    _____ Thermal insulation <u>negates</u> the effect of the cold.

    _____ The governor issued a statement in an attempt to <u>negate</u> the accusations against him.

Vocabulary Builder 8 Answers

1. **The correct answer is 2/1.**

2. **The correct answer is 2/1.**

3. **The correct answer is 2/1.**

4. **The correct answer is 1/2.**

5. **The correct answer is 1/2.**

6. **The correct answer is 2/1.**

7. **The correct answer is 3/1/2.**

8. **The correct answer is 2/1.**

9. **The correct answer is 2/1.**

10. **The correct answer is 1/2.**

Vocabulary Builder 9

Directions: Select the one word from the choices given that best completes each of these sentences. Write it in the space provided.

NOTE

A rule for the negative prefixes is *il* before *l*; *im* before *b*, *m*, or *p*; *ir* before *r*, and *in* or *un* before other letters.

1. The dying man's speech was so _____ that no one was able to interpret his last request.
   - **(A)** indiscreet
   - **(B)** nonchalant
   - **(C)** incoherent
   - **(D)** impotent

2. Due to many years of _____, the Smiths had nothing to fall back on when it was time for them to retire.
   - **(A)** illiteracy
   - **(B)** impunity
   - **(C)** inflexibility
   - **(D)** imprudence

3. Certain pessimists feel that a nuclear war in our time is _____.
   - **(A)** inevitable
   - **(B)** illicit
   - **(C)** disconcerting
   - **(D)** impossible

4. The personnel manager could not even consider her for the position because of her _____ appearance.
   - **(A)** inept
   - **(B)** inflexible
   - **(C)** unkempt
   - **(D)** disheartened

5. We received the _____ news today that there would be no raises this year.
   - **(A)** disreputable
   - **(B)** uncanny
   - **(C)** incongruous
   - **(D)** disconcerting

6. It was truly miraculous that the child was _____ after falling six stories.

   (A) unscathed

   (B) uncanny

   (C) irreparable

   (D) illiterate

7. Modern architecture often seems _____ in a city rich in history.

   (A) unlikely

   (B) unwitting

   (C) incongruous

   (D) unkempt

8. Serpico is known for his _____ efforts to expose fellow police officers who accepted bribes.

   (A) incalculable

   (B) inexorable

   (C) unwieldy

   (D) illicit

9. Barbara's parents received a report from her teacher that said, "Barbara is an excellent student, but she talks to her friends _____ during class."

   (A) ineptly

   (B) incoherently

   (C) unerringly

   (D) incessantly

10. A civil war pits brother against brother and causes _____ harm to a nation's morale.

    (A) uncompromising

    (B) incalculable

    (C) invariable

    (D) infallible

Vocabulary Builder 9 Answers

1. **The correct answer is (C).**

2. **The correct answer is (D).**

3. **The correct answer is (A).**

4. **The correct answer is (C).**

5. **The correct answer is (D).**

6. **The correct answer is (A).**

7. The correct answer is (C).

8. The correct answer is (B).

9. The correct answer is (D).

10. The correct answer is (B).

Vocabulary Builder 10

Directions: Write the number of the word in Column B that has the same meaning as the word in Column A. Put the number on the line provided.

A	B
_____ **a.** sure	1. inexorable
_____ **b.** unable to do things	2. imprudent
_____ **c.** unharmed	3. incoherent
_____ **d.** inflexible	4. incongruous
_____ **e.** unwise, not careful	5. disreputable
_____ **f.** forbidden	6. infallible
_____ **g.** disjointed, garbled	7. incessant
_____ **h.** not neat	8. illiterate
_____ **i.** very great	9. incalculable
_____ **j.** of bad character	10. disconcerted
_____ **k.** unable to read and write	11. illicit
_____ **l.** inappropriate	12. inept
_____ **m.** constant	13. unscathed
_____ **n.** upset	14. inevitable
_____ **o.** unavoidable	15. unkempt

Vocabulary Builder 10 Answers

a. The correct answer is 6.
b. The correct answer is 12.
c. The correct answer is 13.
d. The correct answer is 1.
e. The correct answer is 2.
f. The correct answer is 11.
g. The correct answer is 3.
h. The correct answer is 15.
i. The correct answer is 9.
j. The correct answer is 5.
k. The correct answer is 8.
l. The correct answer is 4.
m. The correct answer is 7.
n. The correct answer is 10.
o. The correct answer is 14.

EXERCISES: ANTONYMS

Directions: Choose the word among the four alternatives that is the *opposite* (antonym) of the underlined word.

1. I ate lunch with a most <u>convivial</u> group of my friends.
   - (A) lively
   - (B) large
   - (C) unsociable
   - (D) old

2. I prefer <u>muted</u> colors in my living room.
   - (A) changeable
   - (B) bright
   - (C) dull
   - (D) mauve

3. She came for Christmas <u>laden</u> with gifts for everyone.
   - (A) later
   - (B) provided
   - (C) unloaded
   - (D) lifted

4. She had a <u>cozy</u> little apartment in Boston.
   - (A) uncomfortable
   - (B) dirty
   - (C) lazy
   - (D) warm

5. She was a very <u>superficial</u> person with a large group of frivolous friends.
   - (A) superior
   - (B) deep
   - (C) attractive
   - (D) horrible

6. The convicted robber hoped the judge would give him a <u>lenient</u> sentence.
   - (A) easy
   - (B) unmerciful
   - (C) acute
   - (D) frightening

7. Hector takes his dates to <u>intimate</u> restaurants where there is candlelight.
   - (A) large and brightly lit
   - (B) quiet
   - (C) noisy
   - (D) dark

8. As he lay dying, his speech was <u>incoherent</u>.
   - (A) inaudible
   - (B) organized
   - (C) interesting
   - (D) indecent

9. If you want to make a good impression on my father, you will have to be less <u>unkempt</u> than you are now.
   - (A) discreet
   - (B) uncanny
   - (C) literate
   - (D) neat

10. His career in the <u>illicit</u> drug trade ended with the police raid this morning.
    - (A) irregular
    - (B) legal
    - (C) elicited
    - (D) secret

11. Having planned our weekends to watch football, we found the news of the players' strike most <u>disconcerting</u>.

    (A) pleasing

    (B) activating

    (C) refreshing

    (D) debilitating

12. A frightening number of <u>illiterate</u> students are graduating from college.

    (A) able to read and write

    (B) able to enjoy intramural sports

    (C) unable to pass an examination in reading and writing

    (D) inflexible

13. John was so <u>insubordinate</u> that he lost his job within a week.

    (A) fresh

    (B) understanding

    (C) indiscreet

    (D) obedient

14. I cannot stand professors who think they are <u>infallible</u>.

    (A) imperfect

    (B) inexorable

    (C) inept

    (D) inflexible

15. My brother-in-law talks <u>incessantly</u>.

    (A) indiscreetly

    (B) inevitably

    (C) seldom

    (D) sensibly

exercises

EXERCISES: MEANING FROM CONTEXT

Directions: Select a word from the list below that best completes the following sentences.

compete	vast
chagrin	affluent
innovation	lucrative
amenities	rejuvenated
apathy	stereotype

1. The use of audiovisual materials in foreign language teaching was one of the most important _____s in recent years.

2. _____ Middle Easterners have been buying some of England's ancient estates.

3. Wearing his ten-gallon hat, the Texan has become the _____ of the American Westerner.

4. Doing volunteer work at the hospital is not a very _____ pastime.

5. You have made a(n) _____ improvement in your handwriting since you took that calligraphy course.

6. In order to _____ in today's market, we are going to lower our prices.

7. Mrs. Golightly had cosmetic surgery and appears much _____.

8. Imagine his _____ when he discovered he had forgotten to pay his electric bill and the company turned off his power.

9. The automatic washing machine is one of the _____ without which I cannot live.

10. Many a crime has gone unpunished because of the _____ of bystanders.

EXERCISES: SYNONYMS

Directions: Choose the best synonym for the underlined word.

1. She was overcome by <u>chagrin</u> at the check-out counter when she discovered she had left her wallet at home.

    (A) anger

    (B) poverty

    (C) embarrassment

    (D) challenge

2. The space shuttle covered <u>vast</u> distances.

    (A) very

    (B) huge

    (C) varying

    (D) hard

3. Dr. Jones suggested that final examinations be discontinued, an <u>innovation</u> I heartily support.

    (A) entrance

    (B) change

    (C) inner part

    (D) test

4. She plans to <u>compete</u> in the marathon.

    (A) contend

    (B) compare

    (C) delay

    (D) register

5. His new yacht is certainly an <u>ostentacious</u> display of his wealth.

    (A) ossified

    (B) showy

    (C) large

    (D) expensive

6. The doctor warned her that adequate diet was of <u>paramount</u> importance in effecting a cure.

    (A) moving

    (B) chief

    (C) healing

    (D) saving

7. Occasionally, the most unlikely people manage to <u>collaborate</u> successfully.

    (A) put together

    (B) stand together

    (C) work together

    (D) get together

8. Peter advised his <u>clientele</u> that he would be on vacation for the month of January.

    (A) clinic

    (B) customers

    (C) salespeople

    (D) contact

9. I'd rather stay in a hotel with all the <u>amenities</u> than camp in the woods.

    (A) conveniences

    (B) friends

    (C) expenses

    (D) sports

10. The night before this exam I tried not to <u>succumb</u> to sleep.

    (A) scoff

    (B) save

    (C) yield

    (D) try

11. He inherited a <u>lucrative</u> business from his father.

   (A) lucid
   (B) wealthy
   (C) losing
   (D) profitable

12. <u>Apathy</u> toward his studies prevented his graduation.

   (A) indirection
   (B) indifference
   (C) indecision
   (D) indication

13. Her large weight loss has <u>rejuvenated</u> her.

   (A) slimmed again
   (B) subjugated again
   (C) made young again
   (D) made comfortable again

14. Her early skill with numbers was <u>indicative</u> of a genius in mathematics.

   (A) giving direction
   (B) giving indication
   (C) giving assistance
   (D) giving approval

15. Do you think your question is <u>pertinent</u> to the matter we are discussing?

   (A) perceptive
   (B) appropriate
   (C) discriminating
   (D) apparent

16. Although he knew she had work to do, he tried to <u>entice</u> her to go to the beach.

   (A) trace
   (B) enervate
   (C) tempt
   (D) thrice

17. Having spent all my money on tuition, I am not <u>affluent</u> enough even to go to the movies.

   (A) destitute
   (B) arrogant
   (C) wealthy
   (D) afraid

18. A domineering husband, he is the <u>stereotype</u> of a male chauvinist.

   (A) musician
   (B) fixed conception
   (C) disagreeable type
   (D) opposite

19. The senator formerly supported the president's budget plans <u>ardently</u>.

   (A) expertly
   (B) zealously
   (C) arduously
   (D) entirely

20. The hurricane caused great <u>havoc</u> in the islands.

   (A) winds
   (B) treatment
   (C) destruction
   (D) immersion

EXERCISES: PUTTING IT TOGETHER

Directions: This crossword puzzle is a review of the vocabulary used in this chapter.

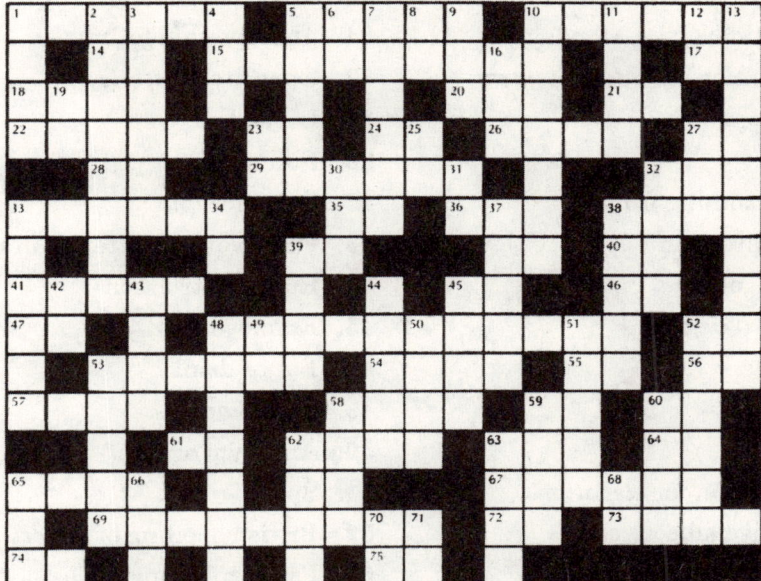

Across

1. Powerful
5. Adjust
10. Eager
14. Prefix meaning *out*
15. Praise
17. Either/_____
18. Synonym for *kind, type*
20. Prefix meaning *nine*
21. Suffix meaning *person who does something*
22. Triplets
23. Neuter pronoun
24. Abbrev. for *Rhode Island*
26. Camper's "house"
27. Abbreviation for *place*
28. Prefix meaning *not*
29. Cause to have no effect
32. Prefix meaning *three*

Down

1. Suffix meaning after
2. Very bad
3. Make longer, increase
4. Prefix meaning *three*
5. Severe
6. Auxiliary verb
7. Neither moral nor immoral
8. Afternoon
9. Deca
10. Acting against
11. Musical piece for two
12. Antonym of *yes*
13. Speaking three languages
16. Someone illiterate is _____ literate.
19. Exclamation
23. Negative prefix used with *coherent*
25. _____ rained last night.
27. Prefix meaning *for*

exercises

Across

33. Abbreviation for *small bedroom*
35. Prefix meaning *not*
36. Negatives
38. Fierce animal
39. Preposition: _____ Monday
40. Abbreviation for *advertisement*
41. Very poor
45. Exist
46. Prefix meaning *from*
47. Neuter pronoun
48. Work together
52. Advanced degree
53. Delicious
54. Huge
55. Article
56. Abbreviation for *elevation*
57. Possessive adjective
58. Slang for *doctors*
59. Prefix meaning *two*
60. Preposition: _____ home
61. _____ soon _____ possible
62. Foot covering
63. Decade
64. Abbreviation for *near*
65. Troubles
67. Tempt
69. Pay back
72. Adverb suffix
73. Where a bird lives
74. Someone who is penniless has _____ money
75. Abbreviation for *street*

Down

30. Alcoholic drink
31. _____tire, whole
32. Rise and fall of the sea
33. Condition of being sane
34. Abbreviation for *mister*
37. Opposite of *subtle*
38. Loaded
39. Full of oil
42. Latin for *and*
43. First word in letter salutation
44. Ruin, destruction
45. Employer
48. Eat or drink
49. See 17 across
50. Antonym of *front*
51. Spoil
52. British spelling of *meters*
53. Prefix meaning *above*
58. Someone who does things
59. Another definition for 29 across
60. Suffix meaning *relating to*
62. Hurt your toe
63. _____ the truth
65. Antonym of *lose*
66. Use the eyes
68. Preposition: _____ January
70. Abbreviation for *Social Security*
71. Abbreviation for *extra-terrestrial*

ANSWER KEY

Antonyms

1.	C	6.	B	11.	A
2.	B	7.	A	12.	A
3.	C	8.	B	13.	D
4.	A	9.	D	14.	A
5.	B	10.	B	15.	C

Meaning from Context

1.	innovation	6.	compete
2.	Affluent	7.	rejuvenated
3.	stereotype	8.	chagrin
4.	lucrative	9.	amenities
5.	vast	10.	apathy

Synonyms

1.	C	8.	B	15.	B
2.	B	9.	A	16.	C
3.	B	10.	C	17.	C
4.	A	11.	D	18.	B
5.	B	12.	B	19.	B
6.	B	13.	C	20.	C
7.	C	14.	B		

Putting It Together

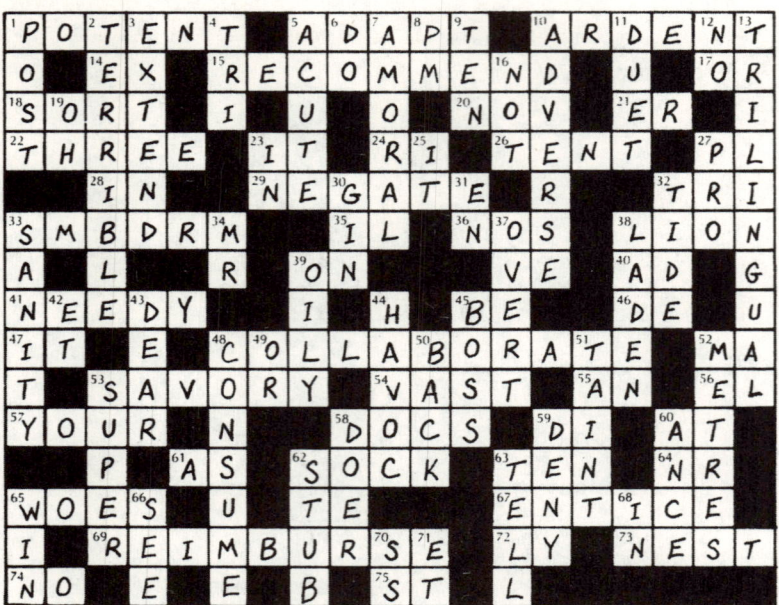

SUMMING IT UP

- If you come across an unusual word, the definition of the word may be close to it.

- Try to understand the definition and apply it to the word in context.

- Every time you read, practice looking for contextual clues.

Everyday and Specific Vocabulary

chapter 4

OVERVIEW

- **Strategies for learning related words**
- **How thoughts are related**
- **Summing it up**

STRATEGIES FOR LEARNING RELATED WORDS

Learning vocabulary in sets of words that are related to each other makes it easier for you to learn the words. It makes your study more structured than learning words in a random way. It also gives you a clue to the meaning of an unknown word. For example, when you see the term "check out" under the subject "library," you will realize it is something you do when you are in a library.

- You should make lists of words that are related to one subject to help you remember them. Keep adding to the list as you learn another word that's related to that area.

- Use a technique that will help you remember the words. You may memorize them or use visual or other clues to help you remember.

- Words related to people and places are tested in the short dialogues and also appear in the longer conversations in the Listening Comprehension section of the TOEFL.

- In the TOEFL short dialogues, you should listen for the word that will be a clue to either the person's occupation or the location.

HOW THOUGHTS ARE RELATED

In addition to providing you with a thorough review, this section of readings will concentrate on thought relations within sentences, paragraphs, and longer passages. It is important to be able to recognize and understand signal words or *connectives*, which introduce, connect, order, and relate individual ideas to larger and often more general concepts.

Study these connectives, paying close attention to their function.

Connectives	Function
and, also, as well as, besides, finally, furthermore, in addition to, in conclusion, moreover	more information will follow
examples, for example, kinds, types, sorts, ordinal numbers (1, 2, 3, etc.), others, several, some, such as, the following, ways	examples will follow
even if, however, in spite of, instead of, nevertheless, on the other hand, rather, still, yet, despite	an opposite idea will follow
all but, except	exceptions will follow
as a result of, because, due to, in order to, on account of, since	cause
as a consequence, as a result, consequently, so, so as to, so that, therefore	effect
after, as soon as, before, if, provided that, should, while, without, unless, until, following	conditions to be met
as, before. . .after, like some. . .other, than, once. . .now	comparison

Look at the following example. Note that the connectives are underlined and the ideas connected are circled. Can you determine the function of each connective? If necessary, refer back to the table.

    Mr. Green had sent his secretary to pick up his car, which he had taken to the garage <u>in order to</u> have the brakes repaired. While returning with Mr. Green's car, the secretary, driving on Main Street, entered the intersection at Elm after the light changed from green to red. She sounded her horn <u>but nevertheless</u> collided with a car that had entered the intersection from Elm Street after the light had turned green.

As you read the following passage, underline the signal words and circle the related ideas. Then give the function of each.

    When a death occurs, the family has religious, social, and legal responsibilities. If the deceased has left an explicit set of papers in an accessible file, arrangements will be much easier for the family to make. For example, such papers should include the deed for a burial plot (if there is one), a statement as to whether cremation or burial is desired, a copy of the birth certificate, and the names and addresses of all family members and friends who should be notified. Furthermore, the papers should include information on bank accounts, safe deposit boxes, and insurance policies, as well as the will. The person in charge of the funeral will need to know how much money is available in order to determine the expenses he or she may reasonably incur for the family.

If feasible, the person who makes the funeral arrangements should not be one of the bereaved. A melancholy widow may not be able to make objective decisions regarding expenses, such as for a coffin. Whoever makes the funeral arrangements realizes that he or she is deputized to make legally binding contracts with a funeral director and others, which will probably be honored some months later when funds from the estate are released.

One of the duties of the person in charge of the funeral is to prepare a death notice for the newspapers. Often the mortician arranges for the insertion of the notice. Included in the information should be the date of death, the names of the family members, and the time and place of the forthcoming interment.

Vocabulary Builder 1

Directions: Choose the correct synonym for the following underlined words.

1. The <u>deceased</u> left you all of her jewelry.
   - (A) missing person
   - (B) dead person
   - (C) wealthy person
   - (D) relative

2. She left <u>explicit</u> instructions regarding her burial.
   - (A) vague
   - (B) exciting
   - (C) irregular
   - (D) clear

3. Because the information was easily <u>accessible</u>, we found it immediately.
   - (A) acceptable
   - (B) accessory
   - (C) reachable
   - (D) probable

4. Property <u>deeds</u> belong in a safe-deposit box.
   - (A) actions
   - (B) legal papers
   - (C) wills
   - (D) addresses

5. He was careful not to <u>incur</u> too many bills for the widow to pay.
    (A) inquire
    (B) pay
    (C) acquire
    (D) change

6. A funeral is a <u>melancholy</u> event.
    (A) meaningful
    (B) medical
    (C) expensive
    (D) sorrowful

7. The family <u>deputized</u> a close friend to make the funeral arrangements.
    (A) disputed
    (B) deprived
    (C) delegated
    (D) dispatched

8. The funeral director gave the <u>death notice</u> to the local newspaper.
    (A) obituary
    (B) funeral
    (C) burial
    (D) biography

9. The <u>undertaker</u> waited three months after the funeral for his bill to be paid.
    (A) tax collector
    (B) beginner
    (C) mortician
    (D) priest

10. In tropical countries, the <u>interment</u> takes place within 24 hours of a death.
    (A) intermittent
    (B) burial
    (C) mourning period
    (D) interruption

Vocabulary Builder 1 Answers

1. The correct answer is (B).
2. The correct answer is (D).
3. The correct answer is (C).
4. The correct answer is (B).
5. The correct answer is (C).
6. The correct answer is (D).
7. The correct answer is (C).
8. The correct answer is (A).
9. The correct answer is (C).
10. The correct answer is (B).

Now try to find the signal words and their functions in the following paragraph.

> The Central Park Conservancy raised $39,000 in private donations to employ twenty-five high school students from the New York area. With commendable zeal, the participants are embellishing the park, as well as weeding and cleaning unkempt areas. Although their employment is merely interim work over the summer, the youths share an affinity for horticulture. Collaboration with the Conservancy only whets their appetites for further endeavors with nature and ecology.

Vocabulary Builder 2

Directions: Choose the word that best completes the sentence.

1. John and Mary _____ on all their books; she writes the text and he does the artwork.
   - (A) study
   - (B) collaborate
   - (C) discuss
   - (D) divide

2. His efforts to keep the peace were so _____ that he was awarded the Nobel Peace Prize.
   - (A) lucrative
   - (B) mercenary
   - (C) commendable
   - (D) heavy

3. They worked from dawn to dusk with such _____ that they were exhausted.
   - **(A)** boredom
   - **(B)** detraction
   - **(C)** debility
   - **(D)** zeal

4. Before they sold their house, they spent two months _____ it.
   - **(A)** trying
   - **(B)** embellishing
   - **(C)** sifting
   - **(D)** planting

5. The _____ in the program were high school students.
   - **(A)** donations
   - **(B)** endeavors
   - **(C)** gardens
   - **(D)** participants

6. In the _____ between shows, the actress went to Paris.
   - **(A)** rush
   - **(B)** closing
   - **(C)** interim
   - **(D)** practice

7. He felt such a close _____ for animals that he became a veterinarian.
   - **(A)** distaste
   - **(B)** affinity
   - **(C)** approach
   - **(D)** likeness

8. A bite of chocolate cake only _____ my desire for more.
   - **(A)** spares
   - **(B)** lets
   - **(C)** changes
   - **(D)** whets

9. Working in the park stimulates his interest in _____.
   - **(A)** archaeology
   - **(B)** horticulture
   - **(C)** zoology
   - **(D)** biology

10. We'll have to clean up this _____ yard before the guests arrive.

    (A) tired

    (B) unlikely

    (C) undone

    (D) unkempt

Vocabulary Builder 2 Answers

1. **The correct answer is (B).**

2. **The correct answer is (C).**

3. **The correct answer is (D).**

4. **The correct answer is (B).**

5. **The correct answer is (D).**

6. **The correct answer is (C).**

7. **The correct answer is (B).**

8. **The correct answer is (D).**

9. **The correct answer is (B).**

10. **The correct answer is (D).**

Here is a longer passage. Look at the first sentence. Can you guess what the article is about?

Before you do the vocabulary builder that follows the reading, locate all the signal words and determine their functions. You will probably find that this will help you achieve a better understanding of the information included here.

Divorce settlements attempt to make an equitable distribution of a couple's assets. Wrangles are common over who gets the car, the furniture, or the dog, but people overlook future needs and income. Two important issues will have to be decided by the courts. Can the divorced wife continue to have health coverage under her former husband's policy? Is the divorced wife entitled to a share of her ex-husband's pension?

So far the subject of health insurance has created much dissension. Most insurance companies exclude former wives from their definition of a worker's dependents. In order to circumvent his ex-wife's exclusion from his health plan, many a husband has concealed his divorce from his employer. Divorced spouses of military men anticipate that a newly approved bill will allow them 180 days' medical coverage and continued coverage for serious ailments if they were married for at least 20 years during their husbands' service career.

Ex-wives are faring better in the pension-sharing dilemma than they are in obtaining health coverage. The courts have set a precedent in awarding pension funds to divorced women, particularly if there are defaults in alimony and child-support payments. Nevertheless, the Employee Retirement Income Security Act prohibits the payment of a pension to anyone other than the worker. Litigation of ex-wives seeking a share in their former husbands' pensions contends that the

ERISA was passed for the purpose of protecting workers from creditors' attempts to attach pensions, not from their ex-wives. In a recent decision, the Supreme Court gave exclusive pension rights to the military retiree whose retirement plan is not under the jurisdiction of state property laws. On the other hand, the former wives of retired foreign service personnel are legally entitled to a share of these retirees' pensions in proportion to the length of their marriage.

Obviously, there is no panacea for the ills besetting the legal system. Divorced women can only pray for significant benefits from future legislation.

Vocabulary Builder 3

Directions: In this exercise, put the number of the synonym in Column B beside the word in Column A.

A	B
_____ **a.** equitable	**1.** illness
_____ **b.** assets	**2.** example
_____ **c.** wrangle	**3.** cure
_____ **d.** ailment	**4.** quarrel
_____ **e.** fare	**5.** succeed
_____ **f.** dilemma	**6.** impartial
_____ **g.** precedent	**7.** property
_____ **h.** default	**8.** fail
_____ **i.** panacea	**9.** predicament

Answers

a. The correct answer is 6.

b. The correct answer is 7.

c. The correct answer is 4.

d. The correct answer is 1.

e. The correct answer is 5.

f. The correct answer is 9.

g. The correct answer is 2.

h. The correct answer is 8.

i. The correct answer is 3.

Vocabulary Builder 4

In this group of words, the noun is formed by adding *ion* to the verb. Note the spelling change in some of them.

Verb	Noun
anticipate	anticipation
celebrate	celebration
circumvent	circumvention
direct	direction
donate	donation
exhilarate	exhilaration
insert	insertion
intimidate	intimidation
legislate	legislation
litigate	litigation
object	objection
participate	participation
select	selection

If there are any words that you do not understand from the list above, look them up in your dictionary. Then, select the word from the four choices that best completes the sentence. Write the correct form in the space provided.

1. Recent _____ has raised taxes on luxury items.

   object   celebrate   legislate   donate

2. Half the enjoyment of a vacation is the _____ of it.

   insert   direct   object   anticipate

3. Unless a will is written clearly, _____ among family members may be inevitable.

   legislate   litigate   celebrate   select

4. I hope you don't _____ to my smoking.

   intimidate   participate   circumvent   object

5. Americans _____ the Fourth of July with a bang.

   donate   celebrate   direct   legislate

6. We were surprised by the _____ of candidates for the legislature.

   insert   anticipate   direct   select

7. The police department _____ trouble at the antinuclear demonstration this afternoon.

   object   anticipate   participate   circumvent

8. It is difficult to _____ additional material in a manuscript once it has been prepared for the printer.

    insert   direct   donate   celebrate

9. He gave a generous _____ to the public television station.

    donate   celebrate   participate   direct

10. Thousands of runners _____ in the annual Boston Marathon.

    celebrate   exhilarate   intimidate   participate

Vocabulary Builder 4 Answers

1. **The correct answer is legislation.**

2. **The correct answer is anticipation.**

3. **The correct answer is litigation.**

4. **The correct answer is object.**

5. **The correct answer is celebrate.**

6. **The correct answer is selection.**

7. **The correct answer is anticipates.**

8. **The correct answer is insert.**

9. **The correct answer is donation.**

10. **The correct answer is participate.**

Vocabulary Builder 5

Directions: Choose the correct synonym for the underlined word in the following sentences. Use your dictionary if you need to.

1. Tom insisted upon a fair <u>share</u> of the partnership's profits.

    (A) spare

    (B) division

    (C) merit

    (D) help

2. The president held a <u>brief</u> press conference.

    (A) documented

    (B) long

    (C) pleasant

    (D) short

3. In spite of his rude behavior on the tennis court, John has many <u>ardent</u> admirers.
    - (A) arduous
    - (B) eager
    - (C) wild
    - (D) fabulous

4. An affable response frequently turns away <u>wrath</u>.
    - (A) pleasant
    - (B) loud
    - (C) polite
    - (D) angry

5. It is extremely hazardous to try to break up a <u>fierce</u> dog fight.
    - (A) cross
    - (B) ravenous
    - (C) noisy
    - (D) violent

6. <u>Superstition</u> may easily lead you astray.
    - (A) irrational belief
    - (B) succession
    - (C) logic
    - (D) misdirection

7. Queen Victoria's <u>palatial</u> country home draws many visitors to the Isle of Wight.
    - (A) palatine
    - (B) paltry
    - (C) palace-like
    - (D) partial

8. The little boy certainly has distinguished <u>godparents</u>.
    - (A) mother and father
    - (B) sponsors at the baptism
    - (C) religious supporters
    - (D) loving relatives

9. The principal threatened to <u>expel</u> him from school if he didn't behave better.
   - **(A)** excise
   - **(B)** exert
   - **(C)** send out
   - **(D)** try out

10. He sang the hymn to the <u>accompaniment</u> of the church choir.
    - **(A)** voices
    - **(B)** support
    - **(C)** meter
    - **(D)** music

Vocabulary Builder 5 Answers

1. **The correct answer is (B).**
2. **The correct answer is (D).**
3. **The correct answer is (B).**
4. **The correct answer is (A).**
5. **The correct answer is (D).**
6. **The correct answer is (A).**
7. **The correct answer is (C).**
8. **The correct answer is (B).**
9. **The correct answer is (C).**
10. **The correct answer is (B).**

Vocabulary Builder 6

Directions: Now use the vocabulary words to complete these sentences. Be sure to use the correct form.

1. The spy was hanged for _____ with the enemy.
   working together

2. I spend my weekends at my beach house, far from the noise and _____ of the big city.
   overcrowding

3. The defense attorney could not find a witness whose version of the incident _____ with that of the accused.
   agreed

4. Certain drugs have been blamed for _____ defects and should not be prescribed for pregnant women.   before birth

5. The children are making so much noise that I can't _____ on my work.   give complete attention

6. Reading is an essential _____ of any language course.
        part

7. How did you ever come up with that unappetizing _____?
                                        mixture

8. The priest promised to _____ evil and help those in need.
        fight

9. If only we had made sure that we were truly _____ before we made our nuptial vows!   able to live together

10. The decision concerning the withdrawal of troops was made at a _____ between the Attorney General and the President.
    meeting

11. Every morning at nine the boss and her secretary _____ on the work plan for the day.   talk together

12. If he is serious about a career in journalism, he ought to develop a more _____ style of writing.
    short and clear

13. White wine is a _____ to a good seafood dinner.
                    something that completes

14. Thousands of athletes from around the world _____ in the Olympic Games.   try to win

15. Only my older sister knows my secrets; she and I have _____ in each other since we were children.   talked freely

Vocabulary Builder 6 Answers

1. **The correct answer is collaborating.**

2. **The correct answer is congestion.**

3. **The correct answer is concurred.**

4. **The correct answer is congenital.**

5. **The correct answer is concentrate.**

6. **The correct answer is component.**

7. **The correct answer is concoction.**

8. **The correct answer is combat.**

9.   The correct answer is compatible.

10.   The correct answer is conclave.

11.   The correct answer is confer.

12.   The correct answer is concise.

13.   The correct answer is complement.

14.   The correct answer is compete.

15.   The correct answer is confided.

Vocabulary Builder 7

Directions: Choose the alternative that has the *same meaning* as the underlined word.

1.   He reads periodicals that are <u>pertinent</u> to his profession.
      - **(A)** appropriate
      - **(B)** apparent
      - **(C)** perceptive
      - **(D)** discriminating

2.   I like chocolate <u>as well as</u> licorice.
      - **(A)** but the opposite
      - **(B)** in spite of
      - **(C)** and
      - **(D)** rather than

3.   Before Smith went on vacation, he left <u>explicit</u> instructions for the painting of his apartment.
      - **(A)** colorful
      - **(B)** clear
      - **(C)** verbal
      - **(D)** written

4.   I'm looking for a little cabin in the woods where I won't be <u>accessible</u> to my relatives.
      - **(A)** acceptable
      - **(B)** probable
      - **(C)** reachable
      - **(D)** accessory

5. John and Mary worked on their garden with such <u>zeal</u> this summer that they grew more tomatoes than they could eat.

   (A) fertilizers

   (B) garden tools

   (C) unwillingness

   (D) enthusiasm

6. No one could decide whether she married him for <u>mercenary</u> motives or she loved him in spite of his millions.

   (A) money-loving

   (B) mercurial

   (C) unknown

   (D) lucrative

7. Because he had <u>defaulted</u> in his car payments, the bank repossessed the car.

   (A) erred

   (B) deprived

   (C) failed

   (D) delayed

8. Because he had invited two girls to the dance, he found himself in a terrible <u>dilemma</u>.

   (A) predicament

   (B) romance

   (C) argument

   (D) discussion

9. No matter how hard we try, there is no way to <u>circumvent</u> taxes.

   (A) pay in installments

   (B) get around

   (C) travel around

   (D) round up

10. Because their birthdays occurred in the same month, they <u>shared</u> a birthday party.

   (A) celebrated

   (B) spared

   (C) merited

   (D) experienced together

11. He's such an <u>affable</u> fellow that people sometimes take advantage of him.
    (A) accessible
    (B) good-natured
    (C) wealthy
    (D) weak

12. A recent bride enjoys <u>concocting</u> special dinners for her husband.
    (A) putting together
    (B) inventing
    (C) coordinating
    (D) cooperating

13. Married couples can get a divorce if they find they are not <u>compatible</u>.
    (A) able to budget their money
    (B) capable of having children
    (C) capable of living harmoniously
    (D) able to share an apartment or house

14. The <u>consensus</u> among his sisters was that he ought to get married.
    (A) agreement
    (B) survey
    (C) statistics
    (D) concentration

15. The newscaster gave a <u>concise</u> account of the tragedy.
    (A) long and detailed
    (B) sad and depressing
    (C) complicated and intricate
    (D) short and clear

Vocabulary Builder 7 Answers

1. **The correct answer is (A).**

2. **The correct answer is (C).**

3. **The correct answer is (B).**

4. **The correct answer is (C).**

5. **The correct answer is (D).**

6. **The correct answer is (A).**

7. **The correct answer is (C).**

8.   The correct answer is (A).

9.   The correct answer is (B).

10. The correct answer is (D).

11. The correct answer is (B).

12. The correct answer is (A).

13. The correct answer is (C).

14. The correct answer is (A).

15. The correct answer is (D).

Vocabulary Builder 8

Directions: Put the number of the definition or synonym in Column B beside the appropriate word in Column A.

A	B
_____ **a.** stereotype	**1.** move slowly and aimlessly
_____ **b.** meander	**2.** increase
_____ **c.** pilfer	**3.** elementary, initial
_____ **d.** complement	**4.** jubilant song
_____ **e.** amenity	**5.** draw out
_____ **f.** augment	**6.** steal
_____ **g.** paean	**7.** pleasantness
_____ **h.** rudimentary	**8.** fixed pattern representing a type of person
_____ **i.** habitat	**9.** natural locality of plant or animal
_____ **j.** elicit	**10.** make complete

Directions: Use the words above to complete the following sentences.

1.   On Sundays, I love to _____ through the woods and bird watch.

2.   Comprehending calculus is impossible if you have only a _____ knowledge of mathematics.

3.   Wildlife sanctuaries protect the _____ of birds and the plants on which they feed.

4.   Absent-minded and thoughtful, Dr. James is the _____ of a college professor.

5. He will have to find a second job to _____ his income.

6. Vocabulary exercises _____ the work required for reading comprehension.

7. The detective tried to _____ the truth from the captured felon.

8. The superintendent was trying to catch the person who had _____ from the children's desks.

9. The hotel we stayed in last weekend didn't have a single _____ , so we left after one night.

10. At the Thanksgiving service, the congregation sang a _____ .

Vocabulary Builder 8 Answers

a. **The correct answer is 8.**

b. **The correct answer is 1.**

c. **The correct answer is 6.**

d. **The correct answer is 10.**

e. **The correct answer is 7.**

f. **The correct answer is 2.**

g. **The correct answer is 4.**

h. **The correct answer is 3.**

i. **The correct answer is 9.**

j. **The correct answer is 5.**

1. **The correct answer is meander.**

2. **The correct answer is rudimentary.**

3. **The correct answer is habitats.**

4. **The correct answer is stereotype.**

5. **The correct answer is augment.**

6. **The correct answer is complement.**

7. **The correct answer is elicit.**

8. **The correct answer is pilferred.**

9. **The correct answer is amenity.**

10. **The correct answer is paean.**

When reading in English, you will come across foreign words that have been incorporated into the language. Below is a list of some of the most commonly used foreign words. Find out what they mean, add them to your cards, then do the exercises that follow.

1. ad infinitum
2. alumnus, alumna
3. bête noire
4. carte blanche
5. cliché
6. connoisseur
7. coquette
8. coup de grace
9. dilettante
10. double entendre
11. élite
12. ennui
13. rapport
14. faux pas
15. forte
16. gourmet
17. macabre
18. magnum opus
19. misanthrope
20. misogynist
21. non sequitor
22. nouveau riche
23. par excellence
24. parvenu
25. pecadillo
26. potpourri
25. savoir faire
28. suave
29. tyro
30. virtuoso

Now study these sentences that give you examples of how these words are generally used in English sentences.

1. She talked about her troubles *ad infinitum*, so we all went home early.

2. He is an *alumnus* of Boston University, and she is an *alumna* of Princeton.

3. My *bête noire* has always been spelling.

4. The Queen was given *carte blanche* wherever she went.

5. The speaker's lecture was full of *clichés*, which annoyed his audience greatly.

6. As a *connoisseur* of modern art, he was invited to all of the gallery openings.

7. Carmen was a *coquette* whom no man could resist.

8. As far as he was concerned, the *coup de grace* in the divorce settlement was his wife's getting the dog.

9. He will never be anything more than a *dilettante* in art.

10. At the bachelors' party, everything that was said seemed to have a *double entendre*.

11. Only the *élite* were invited to the royal wedding.

12. That movie was so bad that I nearly passed out from *ennui*.

13. It is important for teachers to establish a good *rapport* with their students.

14. Not thanking the hostess for dinner was a *faux pas* on my part.

15. Mathematics is definitely John's *forte*.

16. Charlie's Chophouse is not for *gourmets*.

17. The children were frightened by the *macabre* Halloween decorations.

18. After thirty years of intense work on his *magnum opus*, he found a publisher.

19. His denunciation of just about everyone and everything earned him the reputation of a *misanthrope*.

20. He was so old when he got married that his friends had begun to think that he was a *misogynist*.

21. Helen's conversation is so full of *non sequitors* that we cannot understand her.

22. The neighbors are obviously *nouveau riche* and don't have the vaguest notion of good taste.

23. Perlman is a violinist *par excellence*.

24. A *parvenue*, he was not accepted by the old families of Bar Harbor.

25. His wife was used to his *pecadillos* and forgave them.

26. Stew is a *potpourri* of meat and vegetables.

27. She showed a great deal of *savoir faire* for such a young girl.

28. A *suave* gentleman never lacks invitations to dinner.

29. A *tyro* in the business world usually earns very little money.

30. Wynton Marsalis is a *virtuoso* in the music world.

Vocabulary Builder 9

Directions: Determine the meaning of the underlined word from the context.

1. Students <u>beguile</u> their leisure hours in computer stores.
   - **(A)** cause time to pass unnoticed
   - **(B)** begin
   - **(C)** waste regrettably
   - **(D)** fool around

2. He <u>devised</u> a computer game and sold it to Atari.
   - **(A)** played
   - **(B)** bought
   - **(C)** invented
   - **(D)** divided

3. Manufacturers are <u>donating</u> computers to schools.
   - **(A)** giving
   - **(B)** going
   - **(C)** dedicating
   - **(D)** deducting

4. I am not <u>ingenious</u> enough to invent a video game.
   - **(A)** studious
   - **(B)** clever
   - **(C)** glorious
   - **(D)** indigenous

5. <u>Currently</u>, students appear to be learning and having fun simultaneously.
   - **(A)** electrically
   - **(B)** concurrently
   - **(C)** sometimes
   - **(D)** at the present time

6. It is said that you can <u>intimidate</u> your enemies by speaking in a low voice and carrying a big stick.
   - **(A)** frighten
   - **(B)** attack
   - **(C)** harass
   - **(D)** make peace with

7. <u>Avid</u> opera lovers are willing to stand in line for hours.
   - **(A)** musical
   - **(B)** averse
   - **(C)** eager
   - **(D)** tedious

8. Einstein was a <u>brilliant</u> mathematician.
   - **(A)** shining
   - **(B)** very intelligent
   - **(C)** famous
   - **(D)** foreign

9. A computer may be used in the math classroom to <u>implement</u> the lesson.
   - **(A)** implant
   - **(B)** learn
   - **(C)** entreat
   - **(D)** carry out

10. Physics is an <u>enigma</u> to me.
    (A) energy
    (B) problem
    (C) mystery
    (D) trial

11. A hundred dollars will <u>suffice</u> to buy a home computer.
    (A) be saved
    (B) be charged
    (C) be suffered
    (D) be enough

12. The kids spoke a <u>jargon</u> of their own that no one else understood.
    (A) accent
    (B) unintelligible talk
    (C) vocabulary
    (D) foreign language

13. It was a <u>minute</u> crack in the motor block that ruined the car.
    (A) hidden
    (B) multiple
    (C) many-sided
    (D) very small

14. Studying vocabulary can be an <u>irksome</u> task.
    (A) easy
    (B) pleasant
    (C) tedious
    (D) irate

15. The tennis player protested the call with great <u>fervor</u>.
    (A) passion
    (B) favor
    (C) fever
    (D) dislike

Vocabulary Builder 9 Answers

1. **The correct answer is (A).**

2. **The correct answer is (C).**

3. **The correct answer is (A).**

4. The correct answer is (B).

5. The correct answer is (D).

6. The correct answer is (A).

7. The correct answer is (C).

8. The correct answer is (B).

9. The correct answer is (D).

10. The correct answer is (C).

11. The correct answer is (D).

12. The correct answer is (B).

13. The correct answer is (D).

14. The correct answer is (C).

15. The correct answer is (A).

Vocabulary Builder 10

Directions: Determine the meaning of the underlined word from the context; then select the best synonym.

1. Mr. Morton went downstairs to <u>receive</u> them.
    - **(A)** get
    - **(B)** welcome
    - **(C)** say goodbye to
    - **(D)** sign for

2. Lady Augustus, though <u>economical</u> in most things, spent a lot of money on clothes.
    - **(A)** awkward
    - **(B)** extravagant
    - **(C)** thrifty
    - **(D)** careless

3. They lived <u>luxuriously</u> even though they had no income.
    - **(A)** expensively
    - **(B)** cheaply
    - **(C)** usury
    - **(D)** beautifully

4. Arabella never <u>stirred</u> anywhere without her maid.
    (A) mixed
    (B) moved
    (C) stayed
    (D) resided

5. It would be <u>grievous</u> to her to live without her maid.
    (A) pleasant
    (B) grateful
    (C) painful
    (D) tearful

6. The expensive purse was a necessary <u>appendage</u> to Arabella.
    (A) something added
    (B) application
    (C) dependent
    (D) servant

7. He never <u>betrayed</u> himself to anyone but the butler.
    (A) made known
    (B) fooled
    (C) bewildered
    (D) bestowed

8. She was graceful and never moved <u>awkwardly</u>.
    (A) smoothly
    (B) clumsily
    (C) merrily
    (D) gracefully

9. She <u>prided</u> herself on her graceful walk.
    (A) was proud
    (B) was pricked
    (C) was happy
    (D) was sorry

10. He, on the other hand, always seemed to <u>drag</u>.
    (A) dread to move
    (B) dress carelessly
    (C) walk fast
    (D) move too slowly

11. A woman who marries for money, not love, is indeed <u>mercenary</u>.
    (A) loving money
    (B) disinterested
    (C) responsible
    (D) meticulous

Vocabulary Builder 10 Answers

1. The correct answer is (B).
2. The correct answer is (C).
3. The correct answer is (A).
4. The correct answer is (B).
5. The correct answer is (C).
6. The correct answer is (A).
7. The correct answer is (A).
8. The correct answer is (B).
9. The correct answer is (A).
10. The correct answer is (D).
11. The correct answer is (A).

EXERCISES: SYNONYMS

Directions: Choose the alternative that has the *same meaning* as the underlined word.

1. Before you can take calculus, you need more than a <u>rudimentary</u> knowledge of algebra.

    (A) rude

    (B) thorough

    (C) elementary

    (D) superficial

2. The <u>augmentation</u> in the population has created a fuel shortage.

    (A) augury

    (B) increase

    (C) demand

    (D) necessity

3. Detective Smith used various means to <u>elicit</u> a confession from the murderer.

    (A) make

    (B) force

    (C) frame

    (D) draw out

4. It seems <u>inevitable</u> that the world will end from natural causes.

    (A) invariable

    (B) unavoidable

    (C) impressionable

    (D) inestimable

5. Dr. Salk was <u>lauded</u> for his work with the polio vaccine.

    (A) rewarded

    (B) merited

    (C) praised

    (D) heralded

6. The spacecraft <u>orbited</u> the earth many times.

    (A) circled

    (B) viewed

    (C) returned

    (D) overlooked

7. Dick met Jane at a secluded <u>rendezvous</u> overlooking the avenue.

    (A) restaurant

    (B) park

    (C) meeting place

    (D) picnic ground

8. <u>Dauntless</u> men and women crossed America in covered wagons.

    (A) foreign

    (B) fearless

    (C) adventuresome

    (D) penniless

9. The pilot miraculously survived the crash <u>unscathed</u>.

    (A) unsurprised

    (B) unhurt

    (C) unhappy

    (D) undeterred

10. A week's <u>sojourn</u> in Paris can be very expensive.

    (A) shopping

    (B) sightseeing

    (C) journey

    (D) stay

11. A younger sister is <u>obnoxious</u> to have around when the older sister's boyfriend comes to the house.

    (A) welcome

    (B) too much

    (C) objectionable

    (D) talkative

12. You should try to avoid <u>clichés</u> if you want to be a creative writer.

    (A) ungrammatical sentences

    (B) improper language

    (C) plagiarized sections

    (D) trite phrases

13. He <u>devised</u> a folding toothbrush for travelers.

    (A) sold

    (B) bought

    (C) invented

    (D) described

14. The Sphinx was an <u>enigma</u> to all but Oedipus.

    (A) mystery

    (B) problem

    (C) enemy

    (D) entity

15. As an <u>alumnus</u> of Harvard, he felt compelled to contribute to the building fund.

    (A) student

    (B) professor

    (C) supporter

    (D) graduate

exercises

EXERCISES: PUTTING IT TOGETHER

Directions: Try to do this crossword puzzle; it is a review of the vocabulary used in previous chapters.

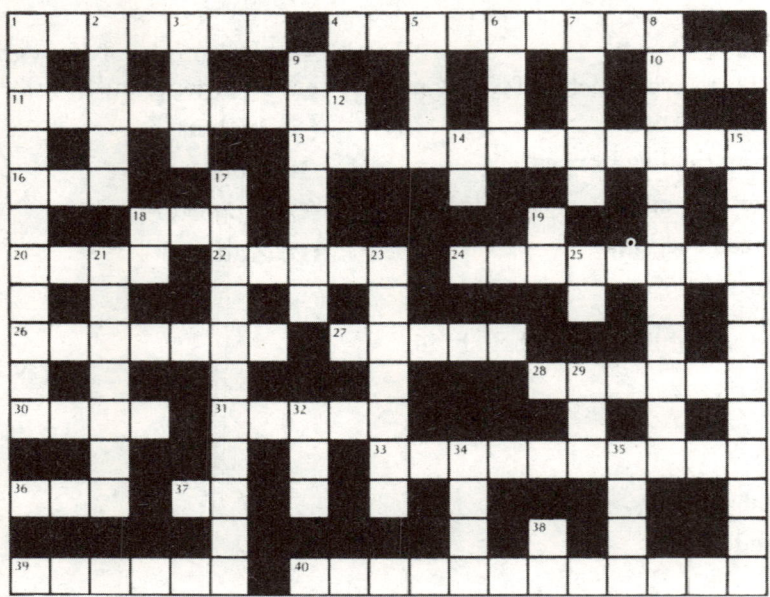

Across

1. Studies or looks at again
4. Make more beautiful
10. Prefix meaning *eight*
11. Delegated
13. Works together
16. Short form of *middle*
18. Hexa
20. Bends the head to show agreement
22. Confusion
24. Ability
26. Friendly, pleasant
27. Feeling of boredom, weariness
28. Kidnap
30. Possessive adjective
31. Salary increase

Down

1. Elementary
2. Dull, uninteresting
3. Consumes
5. Deep, round container
6. Animal used for wool
7. Prefix meaning *between*
8. Science of growing fruit, vegetables, and flowers
9. Antonym of *give*
12. Auxiliary verb
14. Preposition: _____ school
15. Irrational belief
17. Excites
18. Abbreviation for *Social Security*
19. Neuter pronoun
21. Fail, as in payments

Across

33. Avoid by going around
36. Past of *sit*
37. Abbreviation for *saint*
38. Indefinite article
39. Property *who practices*
40. Threaten, making someone act through fear

Down

23. Join together
25. _____ I were you. . .
29. Vagabond
32. Suffix indicating *someone*
34. Wander aimlessly
35. Very large
38. Classified _____

exercises

ANSWER KEY

Synonyms

1. C	6. A	11. C
2. B	7. C	12. D
3. D	8. B	13. C
4. B	9. B	14. A
5. C	10. D	15. D

Putting It Together

SUMMING IT UP

- Make a list of words that relate to each other.
- Words that relate to people and places are usually tested in the short dialogues.
- Words that relate to people and places appear in the longer conversations in the Listening Comprehension section.

All About Roots

OVERVIEW

- **Word roots**
- **Strategies for learning roots**
- **How roots work**
- **Learning words with Greek roots**
- **Learning words with Latin roots**
- **Summing it up**

WORD ROOTS

The **root** of a word contains the basic meaning. Prefixes and suffixes can be added to a root. For example, the root *cred* means "believe," so the English word "credible" means "believable." Learning the roots of words will help you work out the meaning of words you do not know and will consequenly help you with *all* parts of the TOEFL test. Since there are a great number of roots from which words stem in English, the most common ones are presented in this chapter.

STRATEGIES FOR LEARNING ROOTS

- Most word roots are never used alone. They may have prefixes and suffixes attached to them.

- At first you may not see how a particular word grew from the word root. But when you begin to analyze the word, you will see the connection.

- Once you recognize word roots, you will see connections among many words. This will make it easier for you to understand and remember their meanings.

- Try to learn a number of word roots each day. Review the roots you have learned before and try to use them in speech or writing.

- Every time you look up a word in the dictionary, look at its word root (most roots in English come from Latin or Greek).

chapter 5

HOW ROOTS WORK

Prefixes and Suffixes Are Added to Roots to Create Many Words

For example, the root *vor* means "to eat." If you are a *voracious* (voh-*ray*-shus) eater, you eat a lot of food. In the following examples, the root "vor(e)" is combined with prefixes and suffixes to describe types of eaters in the plant and animal kingdoms.

Cover the last column of the following chart and see how many of these words you can figure out by just knowing the meaning of the root "vor."

Word	Prefix	Meaning	Root	Meaning	Word Definition
carnivore	carni	meat	vor	eat	meat eater
insectivore	insect	bug	vor	eat	bug eater
herbivore	herb	plants	vor	eat	plant eater
granivore	gran	grain	vor	eat	grain eater
frugivore	frug	fruit	vor	eat	fruit eater
graminivore	gram	grass	vor	eat	grass eater
nectarivore	nectar	juice	vor	eat	nectar (juice) eater
omnivore	omni	everything	vor	eat	eats everything

Knowing how the words were created can help you figure out many words you encounter on standardized tests. In addition, you can use these decoding skills to figure out the meaning of all the new words that are created every day.

Here's the basic drill:

Adding a prefix to a root	Adding a suffix to a root
de + hydrate = dehydrate	zoo + *ology* = zoology
hydro + power = hydropower	bronch + *itis* = bronchitis

The following chart shows additional examples of how words are put together. Knowing this process can help you take them apart to define them. Remember: words are like people: it's easy to figure them out . . . once you know their parts.

Prefix	+	Root	+	Suffix	=	New Word	Meaning
re	+	fer	+	al	=	referral	connection
de	+	ter	+	ent	=	deterrent	impediment
re	+	pul	+	sion	=	repulsion	send back
dis	+	pel	+	ed	=	dispelled	driven away
re	+	tract	+	able	=	retractable	draw back
im	+	peril	+	ed	=	imperiled	put in danger
dis	+	credit	+	ed	=	discredited	to cause disbelief
ab	+	duct	+	ed	=	abducted	kidnapped

Even if you can't define a word exactly, recognizing the root will give you a general idea of the word's meaning. For example, if you read the word *geocentric*, knowing the root *geo* would help you figure out that *geocentric* has to do with the center ("centric") of the Earth or Earth as the center.

A Word Can Contain More Than One Root

For example, the word *matrilineal* contains the roots *matri* (mother) and *lineal* (line). Putting it together, you can deduce that matrilineal means "determining ancestry through the female line."

Some Roots Are Words Themselves

For example, the root *term* also means "name or length of time." In a similar way, the root *vent* also means "an opening that allows air to enter." Even though these roots are words, they can still function as roots, as the following chart shows:

Root	Meaning	Suffix	New Word	Meaning
term	name	—ology	terminology	wording
term	name	—agant	termagant	shrewish woman
term	end limit	—inal	terminal	end of a series
term	end limit	—less	termless	not limited

Some Roots Must Be Combined with Other Word Elements to Form Words

Take a look at the examples on the following chart:

Root	Meaning	Suffix	New Word	Meaning	Pronunciation
aud	hear	—ible	audible	able to be heard	(*aw*-di-ble)
capit	head	—al	capital	most important	
carn	flesh	—al	carnal	of the flesh	(*car*-nal)

When It Comes to Building Words from Roots, Placement Matters

Some roots can also function as prefixes, depending on their placement in a word. For example, *graphy* means "writing."

used as a root	*calligraphy*
used as a prefix	*graphology*

TIP

Whenever you come upon an unfamiliar word, first check to see if it has a recognizable root.

Vocabulary Builder 1

Directions: There are fifteen words hidden in this word-find puzzle. Every word begins with "A." To complete the puzzle, locate and circle all the words. The words may be written forward, backward, or upside down.

a	a	a	a	s	s	i	d	u	o	u	s	y	a
q	a	b	h	o	r	k	k	q	q	a	a	r	m
a	b	r	o	g	a	t	e	z	q	s	p	o	p
l	w	d	n	o	c	s	b	a	v	y	o	t	h
u	x	a	d	m	o	n	i	s	h	l	s	a	i
t	n	e	l	a	v	i	b	m	a	u	t	l	b
i	z	e	t	o	d	i	t	n	a	m	l	u	i
o	z	a	n	t	i	p	a	t	h	y	e	b	o
n	v	a	p	p	e	a	s	e	z	z	x	m	u
a	g	g	r	a	n	d	i	z	e	x	x	a	s
h	e	y	a	n	t	i	t	h	e	s	i	s	x

Vocabulary Builder 1 Answers

1. **abhor:** to turn away from; loathe

2. **abrogate:** to repeal; do away with

3. **abscond:** to steal away and hide

4. **admonish:** to strongly urge or caution

5. **aggrandize:** to make more powerful, important, or wealthier

6. **ambivalent:** having conflicting emotions

7. **ambulatory:** able to move

8. **amphibious:** capable of living both on land and in water

9. **antidote:** a remedy against a poison

10. **antipathy:** a strong feeling of dislike; hostility; aversion

11. **antithesis:** a contrast of ideas

12. **apostle:** a person sent away to deliver a message

13. **appease:** to pacify; bring toward peace

14. **assiduous:** diligent; industrious

15. **asylum:** a place of security or retreat

LEARNING WORDS WITH GREEK ROOTS

Many of the words we use every day come from Greek roots. This is especially true of the language of scientific words, because much of the language of science was created primarily from Greek roots. Scientific words often appear on standardized tests.

Greek Roots for Measurement

You'll notice that some of the roots have more than one spelling. For example, *macro* and *mega* both mean "large." Read the following chart over several times and you'll soon get accustomed to the slight variations in spelling.

Root	Meaning	Example	Definition
acr	topmost	acrophobia	fear of high places (ak-roh-*foh*-bee-uh)
arch/ prot	first	archbishop prototype	highest bishop first of its kind
chron	time	chronicle	historical record
ger/ paleo	old	geriatric	relating to old age (ger-ee-*at*-trik) paleogeology the science of Earth's history (pay-lee-oh-gee-*ol*-oh-ge)
horo	hour	horoscope	signs of the zodiac (*hor*-oh-scope)
macro/ mega	large	macroscopic megalith	seen with the naked eye huge stone
meter	measure	altimeter	device to measure altitude (al-*tih*-ma-ter)
micro	small	microbe	tiny organism (*my*-krobe)
morph	form	metamorphosis	change of form (meh-tah-*mor*-foh-sis)
neo	new	neophyte	beginner (*nee*-oh-fite)
pan	all	panacea	a cure-all (pana-*see*-uh)
ped	foot	pedometer	device for measuring steps (peh-*dom*-eh-ter)
poly	many	polyglot	speaking several languages (*poh*-lee-glot)
tele	far off	telescope	device for seeing distant objects

Words with the Hydro/Hydra Root

Many useful words are formed from the hydro/hydra root. The following chart shows some of the most important ones that often appear on standardized tests:

Word	Definition	Pronunciation
hydrostat	electrical device for detecting water	(*hi*-droh-stat)
dehydrate	dry out	(dee-*hi*-drate)
hydrophobia	rabies; literally, *fear of water*	(hi-droh-*foh*-bee-uh)
hydroplane	boat that travels on water	(*hi*-droh-playn)
hydroponics	growing plants in water	(hi-droh-*pon*-iks)
hydropower	power generated from water	(*hi*-droh-pow-ur)
hydrate	combine with water	(*hi*-drate)
hydrangea	flower (that needs much water)	(hi-*drayn*-jah)
hydrotherapy	water therapy	(hi-droh-*ther*-a-pee)
hydrosphere	water on Earth	(*hi*-droh-sfeer)

Words About the Natural World

Below are some Greek roots and words formed from them that concern the natural world.

Root	Meaning	Example	Definition
anthrop	human	anthropology	study of humankind (an-throh-*pol*-oh-gee)
bio	life	biology	the study of life
dem	people	democracy	rule by the people
gen	race	genetics	study of heredity (jen-*eh*-tiks)
		eugenics	improving offspring (yoo-*jen*-iks)
helio	sun	heliotrope	sunflower (*hee*-lee-uh-trop)
ichthy	fish	ichthyology	study of fish (ik-thee-*ol*-oh-gee)
ornith	bird	ornithology	study of birds (or-neh-*thol*-oh-gee)
ped	foot	pedometer	instrument that measures footsteps
phyt	plant	phytology	study of plants (fi-*tol*-oh-gee)
polit	citizen	cosmopolitan	citizen of the world
pyr	fire	pyrogenic	producing heat (pi-roh-*jen*-ik)
soma	body	somatic	physical (sew-*mah*-tik)
thermo	heat	thermostat	device for regulating heat
zoo	animal	zoology	study of animals

Vocabulary Builder 2

Directions: First unscramble each of the seven testworthy words so that it matches its definition. Then, use the words to fill the appropriate spaces on the corresponding line. When you have completed the entire puzzle, you'll see another word vertically in the column with circles.

1. tryooppet	first of its kind	⬭☐☐☐☐☐☐☐☐
2. bldiuae	able to be heard	⬭☐☐☐☐☐☐
3. hpyteeon	beginner	⬭☐☐☐☐☐☐☐
4. iahobroacp	fear of high places	⬭☐☐☐☐☐☐☐☐☐
5. leronichc	historical record	⬭☐☐☐☐☐☐☐☐
6. scnieegu	improving offspring	⬭☐☐☐☐☐☐☐
7. ophbichars	highest bishop	⬭☐☐☐☐☐☐☐☐☐

Vocabulary Builder 2 Answers

1. The correct answer is **prototype**.

2. The correct answer is **audible**.

3. The correct answer is **neophyte**.

4. The correct answer is **acrophobia**.

5. The correct answer is **chronicle**.

6. The correct answer is **eugenics**.

7. The correct answer is **archbishop**.

Word reading down: **panacea**

Greek Roots for Beliefs and Ideas

The Greek roots form many testworthy words that describe beliefs and ideas as well.

How many of the following words do you know? Test yourself by covering the fourth column and trying to define each word.

Root	Meaning	Example	Definition
archy/cracy	rule by	monarchy	rule by a single leader (*mon*-ar-kee)
biblio	book	bibliophile	book lover, book collector (*bib*-lee-oh-file)
dox	belief	orthodox	conforming to approved beliefs
gam	marriage	polygamy	multiple wives (poh-*li*-guh-me)
graph	writing	graphology	study of handwriting (graf-*ol*-oh-gee)
ideo	idea	ideology	body of knowledge (aye-dee-*ol*-oh-gee)
logy	study of	anthropology	study of humanity (an-throh-*pol*-oh-gee)
nom	rule	autonomy	self-rule (aw-*ton*-oh-mee)
onym	name	pseudonym	pen name (*soo*-doh-nim)
orama	view	panorama	complete view (pan-oh-*rah*-muh)
path	feeling	sympathy	compassion
psycho	mind	psychology	study of the mind (si-*col*-oh-gee)
theo	god	theology	study of god (thee-*ol*-oh-gee)
soph	wisdom	sophistry	tricky reasoning (*sof*-is-tree)

Vocabulary Builder 3

Directions: Assess what you've learned so far by completing the following chart. For each word, first write the root and its meaning. Then, use what you've learned about roots to define each word. Don't hesitate to look back at what you just learned—or to use a dictionary.

Word	Root	Meaning	Word Meaning
1. pyrotechnics	_____	_____	_____
2. thermometer	_____	_____	_____
3. gene	_____	_____	_____
4. android	_____	_____	_____
5. zoological	_____	_____	_____
6. thermodynamics	_____	_____	_____
7. politician	_____	_____	_____
8. pyrography	_____	_____	_____
9. engender	_____	_____	_____
10. heliocentric	_____	_____	_____
11. polity	_____	_____	_____
12. zoometry	_____	_____	_____
13. gynarchy	_____	_____	_____
14. ichthyoid	_____	_____	_____
15. ornithopod	_____	_____	_____

Vocabulary Builder 3 Answers

	Word	Root	Meaning	Word Meaning
1.	pyrotechnics	pyro	fire	fireworks
2.	thermometer	thermo	heat	device for measuring heat
3.	gene	gen	race	unit of heredity
4.	android	andr	man	man-shaped robot
5.	zoological	zoo	animal	about animals
6.	thermodynamics	thermo	heat	using heat
7.	politician	polit	citizen	officeholder
8.	pyrography	pyro	fire	burning designs on wood, etc.
9.	engender	gen	race	to produce
10.	heliocentric	helio	sun	relating to the sun as center
11.	polity	polit	citizen	political organization
12.	zoometry	zoo	animal	measuring animals
13.	gynarchy	gyn	women	government by women
14.	ichthyoid	ichthy	fish	fish-like
15.	ornithopod	ornith	bird	bird-like dinosaur

LEARNING WORDS WITH LATIN ROOTS

If you think we've borrowed a lot of roots from the Greeks, wait until you see what we've borrowed from Latin! For example, the Latin root *plac* means "pleasure." Words formed from this root include *placid, complacent, implacable, complaisant,* and *placate.*

The Latin root *nomin/nomen* (name) has given us a great many words, including the following:

Word	Meaning	Pronunciation
ignominious	disgracing one's name	(ig-noh-*min*-ee-us)
misnomer	wrong name	(mis-*noh*-mer)
nomenclature	system of naming	(*noh*-men-clay-ture)
nominal	so-called	(*nom*-in-ul)
nominate	name someone for an office	(*nom*-in-ate)
nominee	candidate	(*nom*-in-ee)

Latin Roots for Size and Amount

Below are fifteen Latin roots that describe size and amount. Study the roots, examples, and definitions. As you read, say the words aloud to help you remember them to use on the TOEFL.

Root	Meaning	Example	Definition
alt	high	altitude	height above surface
ann	year	biannual	happening twice a year
brev	short	brevity	being brief
centr	center	centrist	moderate viewpoint
dors	back	dorsal	back fin
fin/ term	final	finale terminal	the last piece of music (fi-*nal*-ee) end
magni	large	magniloquent	pompous speaking style (mag-*nil*-uh-kwent)
med	middle	median	in the middle (*mee*-dee-an)
multi	many	multifarious	numerous and varied (mul-te-*far*-e-us)
nihil	nothing	annihilate	kill (ann-*ni*-ah-late)
omni	all	omniscient	all-knowing (om-*nish*-ent)
pend	weigh	pendulous	hanging
sed/sess	sit	sedate	quiet
ten/tin	hold	tenet	belief held as true (*tehn*-et)
vid, vis	see	visual	seen (*viz*-yu-al)

Vocabulary Builder 4

Directions: Match the word to its definition. You may wish to underline the Latin root in each word as you do so. Then, write your answers in the space provided.

_____ 1. abdication

_____ 2. diversification

_____ 3. repulsion

_____ 4. benediction

_____ 5. edict

_____ 6. misconduct

_____ 7. viaduct

a. overpass

b. guess

c. variety

d. decree; order

e. renounce a throne

f. assembly; caucus

g. questionable

_____ 8. Congress

_____ 9. conjecture

_____ 10. objectionable

h. aversion

i. wrongdoing

j. blessing

Vocabulary Builder 4 Answers

1. **The correct answer is e.**

2. **The correct answer is c.**

3. **The correct answer is h.**

4. **The correct answer is j.**

5. **The correct answer is d.**

6. **The correct answer is i.**

7. **The correct answer is a.**

8. **The correct answer is f.**

9. **The correct answer is b.**

10. **The correct answer is g.**

Latin Roots for "Kill" or "Cut"

The Latin root *cide* means "kill" or "cut." As you read the following chart, cover the fifth column. See how many words you can decode using what you know about the root and its meaning.

Word	Prefix	Meaning	Root	Word Meaning
insecticide	insect	bug	cide	killing bugs
genocide	gen	people	cide	killing a race of people
homicide	homo	mankind	cide	a person killing a person
matricide	matr	mother	cide	killing your mother
patricide	patr	father	cide	killing your father
fratricide	frat	brother	cide	killing your brother
sororicide	soro	sister	cide	killing your sister
suicide	sui	self	cide	killing yourself
infanticide	infant	baby	cide	killing a baby
ceticide	cet	whales	cide	killing whales

Vocabulary Builder 5

Directions: In the space provided, write **T** if the definition is true and **F** if it is false. Use what you learned about Latin roots to help you figure out what each word means.

_____	1. unification	union
_____	2. degradation	encouragement
_____	3. induce	influence
_____	4. jettison	bring on board
_____	5. addiction	habit; fixation
_____	6. gentrification	growing old
_____	7. scribe	writer
_____	8. malediction	bad luck
_____	9. dejected	depressed
_____	10. propellant	meddler
_____	11. contradict	dissent; deny
_____	12. gradient	flat surface
_____	13. inscribe	write on
_____	14. traduce	praise
_____	15. abduct	kidnap

Vocabulary Builder 5 Answers

1. The correct answer is T.
2. The correct answer is F.
3. The correct answer is T.
4. The correct answer is F.
5. The correct answer is T.
6. The correct answer is F.
7. The correct answer is T.
8. The correct answer is F.
9. The correct answer is T.
10. The correct answer is F.
11. The correct answer is T.
12. The correct answer is F.
13. The correct answer is T.
14. The correct answer is F.
15. The correct answer is T.

Vocabulary Builder 6

Directions: Define each word, using its root to help you. Write your definition on the line provided.

1. compendium _____

2. biannual _____

3. continence _____

4. append _____

5. omniscient _____

6. supersede _____

7. pendulous _____

8. invidious _____

9. secede _____

10. omnivorous _____

Vocabulary Builder 6 Answers

1. **The correct answer is digest; synopsis.**

2. **The correct answer is happening twice a year.**

3. **The correct answer is self-control.**

4. **The correct answer is add.**

5. **The correct answer is perceiving all things.**

6. **The correct answer is go beyond; replace.**

7. **The correct answer is hanging.**

8. **The correct answer is causing resentment.**

9. **The correct answer is withdraw; resign.**

10. **The correct answer is eating all kinds of foods.**

Vocabulary Builder 7

Directions: This list contains a group of miscellaneous verbs whose noun, adjective, or adverb forms do not follow any particular pattern. Use your dictionary if you do not understand the meaning of any of the words. Use the correct form of a word from the list below to complete the sentences below.

Verb	Noun	Adjective	Adverb
abuse	abuse	abusive	abusively
acquire	acquisition		
compare	comparison	comparative	comparatively
damage	damage		
exceed	excess	excessive	excessively
intend	intention	intentional	intentionally
prohibit	prohibition	prohibitive	prohibitively
question	question	questionable	questionably
recommend	recommendation	recommendable	
refuse	refusal		
reply	reply		
require	requirement		
treat	treatment		
use	use, usage	useful	usefully

1. With the President's _____, the bill was passed by Congress.

2. I do not object to the use of alcohol in moderation but, rather, to the _____ use of it.

3. There is a(n) _____ between aspirin and alcohol in this passage.

4. Lincoln's _____ to help the abolitionists incurred their wrath.

5. Send me a list of your _____s for entrance to college.

6. Drug _____ is the subject of this passage.

7. It was not his _____ to take too much aspirin.

8. He had a(n) _____ to ask the professor about the examination.

9. If we have guests for dinner on Saturday, we will _____ our budget for this week.

10. Since the package was insured, the _____ was paid for.

11. _____ was a period in American history when laws prevented legal consumption of alcohol.

12. He was so preoccupied with the _____ of property that he neglected his other interests.

13. There is nothing wrong with the _____ of drugs if you take the proper dosage.

14. His _____ to my letter was short and amusing.

15. Her motives in accepting his proposal are _____.

Vocabulary Builder 7 Answers

1. The correct answer is **recommendation.**

2. The correct answer is **excessive.**

3. The correct answer is **comparison.**

4. The correct answer is **refusal.**

5. The correct answer is **requirement.**

6. The correct answer is **abuse.**

7. The correct answer is **intention.**

8. The correct answer is **question.**

9. The correct answer is **exceed.**

10. The correct answer is **damage.**

11. The correct answer is **Prohibition.**

12. The correct answer is **acquisition.**

14. The correct answer is **use.**

14. The correct answer is **reply.**

15. The correct answer is **questionable.**

Vocabulary Builder 8

Directions: Put the number of the definition in Column B beside the correct word in Column A. There are more definitions than there are words to match.

A	B
_____ **a.** succumb	1. beneath the earth
_____ **b.** sundry	2. relating to treatment of disease
_____ **c.** ensuing	3. various
_____ **d.** underground	4. go up and down
_____ **e.** therapeutic	5. following
_____ **f.** inoculate	6. bend the upper part of the body
_____ **g.** bounce	7. abnormal fear of enclosed space
_____ **h.** adverse	8. die
_____ **i.** despite	9. participate
_____ **j.** claustrophobia	10. inject
	11. unfavorable
	12. in spite of

Vocabulary Builder 8 Answers

a. The correct answer is 8.

b. The correct answer is 3.

c. The correct answer is 5.

d. The correct answer is 1.

e. The correct answer is 2.

f. The correct answer is 10.

g. The correct answer is 4.

h. The correct answer is 11.

i. The correct answer is 12.

j. The correct answer is 7.

Vocabulary Builder 9

Directions: Circle the answer choice that *means the same* as the underlined word.

1. If you know in advance that the examination is going to be easy, you have no <u>incentive</u> to study very much.
   - **(A)** incidence
   - **(B)** motive
   - **(C)** time
   - **(D)** interest

2. When there are severe shortages of fuel, prices <u>soar</u>.
   - **(A)** tower
   - **(B)** slow
   - **(C)** fall
   - **(D)** rise

3. Geraniums thrive if you <u>transplant</u> them from indoors to your garden in the hot weather.
   - **(A)** transfer
   - **(B)** substitute
   - **(C)** trade
   - **(D)** dig

4. The refugees were obliged to <u>halt</u> at the border to have their papers verified.
   - **(A)** hurry
   - **(B)** disrobe
   - **(C)** surrender
   - **(D)** stop

5. Everything I read about costs has the word <u>skyrocketing</u> in it.
   - **(A)** flying in space
   - **(B)** celestial
   - **(C)** writing in the sky
   - **(D)** rapidly increasing

Vocabulary Builder 9 Answers

1. The correct answer is (B).
2. The correct answer is (D).
3. The correct answer is (A).
4. The correct answer is (D).
5. The correct answer is (D).

EXERCISES: SYNONYMS

Directions: Circle the answer choice that has the *same meaning* as the underlined word.

1. Nutritionists believe that vitamins <u>circumvent</u> disease.
   (A) defeat
   (B) nourish
   (C) treat
   (D) feed

2. After his heart attack, Joe went on a <u>therapeutic</u> diet.
   (A) vegetable
   (B) stringent
   (C) curative
   (D) weight-losing

3. Efforts to <u>ameliorate</u> housing conditions for the poor were halted because government funds were cut off.
   (A) add to
   (B) develop
   (C) study
   (D) improve

4. I think your decision to buy the house was <u>judicious</u>.
   (A) extravagant
   (B) wise
   (C) careful
   (D) joyful

5. I have an appointment this afternoon with my <u>chiropodist</u>.
   (A) eye doctor
   (B) skin specialist
   (C) baby doctor
   (D) foot specialist

6. Usually <u>submissive</u>, little Andy suddenly turned rebellious.
   (A) quiet
   (B) obedient
   (C) permissive
   (D) timid

7. Sometimes <u>hyperactive</u> children are given drugs.
   (A) excessively lively
   (B) slow-moving
   (C) very intelligent
   (D) physically disabled

8. Taking college entrance tests with <u>levity</u> is impossible.
   (A) notes
   (B) care
   (C) lightness
   (D) levitation

9. He was <u>notorious</u> among the women for his fickleness.
   (A) infamous
   (B) courted
   (C) famous
   (D) noxious

10. Manufacturers are <u>dubious</u> about predictions of an economic recovery.
    (A) dumbfounded
    (B) delighted
    (C) driven
    (D) doubtful

11. <u>Ostensibly</u>, she enjoys her vacations in Nova Scotia, but she really would prefer someplace warmer.

    (A) probably

    (B) obviously

    (C) seemingly

    (D) definitely

12. Because children are <u>inoculated</u> against measles, there are currently very few cases of the disease in the United States.

    (A) treated

    (B) injected

    (C) isolated

    (D) subjected

13. Pat cannot take elevators because she has <u>claustrophobia</u>.

    (A) unreasonable fear of heights

    (B) unreasonable fear of closed spaces

    (C) unreasonable fear of elevators

    (D) unreasonable fear of people

14. The doctor told him to keep his arm <u>immobile</u> for a few days.

    (A) in a sling

    (B) encased in ice

    (C) motionless

    (D) exercised

15. The hurricane caused <u>incalculable</u> damage in New England.

    (A) very great

    (B) very little

    (C) very calculating

    (D) very abusive

exercises

EXERCISES: PUTTING IT TOGETHER

Directions: This crossword puzzle is a review of some of the vocabulary in this chapter.

<table>
<tr><td>

Across

3. Indefinite article
4. Doubtful
7. Very great
11. Cooking
12. Passive, obedient
14. Go up and down
18. Uncertain
21. Very small
22. Beginner
24. Also
25. Indefinite article
26. Someone who takes part
29. Bring up (children)
30. Past of *feed*

</td><td>

Down

1. Disobedient
2. Stage, platform
3. Suffix meaning *relating to*
5. Antonym of *girls*
6. Abbreviation for *saint*
8. Result
9. Divide into two parts
10. Sickness
13. Signify
15. Equal
16. Death notice
17. Suggests
19. Bother
20. Prefix meaning *many*

</td></tr>
</table>

Across

32. Antonym of *permanent*

35. Shortage

36. Merciless

Down

21. Traveler's tool

23. Suffix meaning *one who*

27. Joyous song

28. Also

30. Temporary pursuit

31. Abbreviation of *definition*

33. Salary

34. Decay

ANSWER KEY

Synonyms

1.	A	6.	B	11.	C
2.	C	7.	A	12.	B
3.	D	8.	C	13.	B
4.	B	9.	A	14.	C
5.	D	10.	D	15.	A

Putting It Together

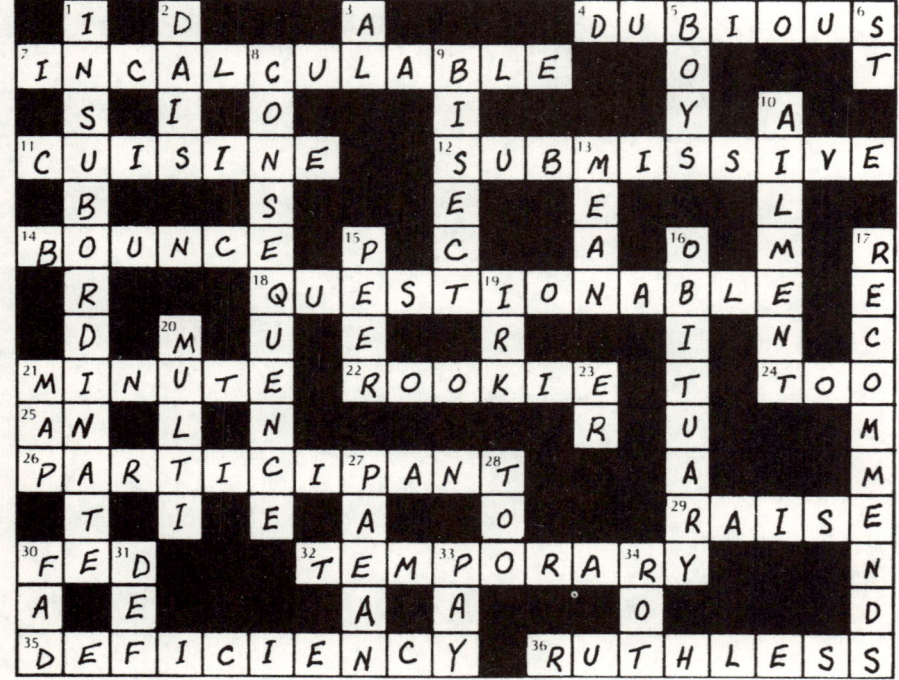

SUMMING IT UP

- Most word roots have prefixes and suffixes attached to them.

- Most roots in English come from Greek or Latin

- You will see connections among words once you recognize the word roots.

All About Prefixes

OVERVIEW

- Prefixes
- Strategies for learning prefixes
- How prefixes work
- Learning words with Greek prefixes
- Learning words with Latin prefixes
- Prefixes for numbers
- Anglo-Saxon prefixes
- Summing it up

PREFIXES

A **prefix** is a form added in front of a word or word root to change its meaning. For example, the prefix *il* means "not," so the word "illegal" means "not legal." Learning prefixes will help you work out the meaning of many words you do not know in English and will help you with all parts of the TOEFL. There are more than fifty prefixes in English and you will learn most of them in this chapter.

STRATEGIES FOR LEARNING PREFIXES

- By doing the vocabulary builders and exercises in this chapter, you will familiarize yourself with the most common prefixes in English. This will enable you to recognize or guess the meanings of hundreds of words.

- A prefix usually changes the meaning of a word. For example, the prefix *in-* changes the meaning of a word to the opposite. "Capable" means "having the ability of doing or being." "Incapable" means "not having the ability of doing or being."

- Prefixes are often attached to roots of words.

Examples		
re	→	act
inter	→	act
trans	→	act

By knowing the prefix and the root, you can work out the meaning of the word.

chapter 6

HOW PREFIXES WORK

Prefixes Are Added to the Front of Roots to Create Many Words

As you have read, prefixes are placed at the beginning of a word to change its meaning. Therefore, knowing just a handful of prefixes can make it easy for you to figure out many words—without ever having to use a dictionary. Here are some examples with the prefix *re*, which means "to do again."

Prefix +	Root =	Word	Definition
re	absorb	reabsorb	absorb again
re	acquaint	reacquaint	meet again
re	qualify	requalify	qualify again
re	admit	readmit	admit again
re	allocate	reallocate	allocate again
re	appear	reappear	appear again
re	arrange	rearrange	change the arrangement
re	attach	reattach	attach again
re	fasten	refasten	fasten again
re	copy	recopy	copy again

Prefixes Are Most Often Attached to Words Without a Break

Even though you may have seen the prefix written with a hyphen (as in *pre-*, *re-*, *de-*), the prefix is attached seamlessly. The following chart shows some examples:

Prefix +	Root =	Word	Definition
dis	inter	disinter	to unearth (dis-in-*tur*)
dis	credit	discredit	to cause to be doubted
extra	terrestrial	extraterrestrial	alien (not of this place)
in	tractable	intractable	hard to handle; unmanageable
mal	content	malcontent	a dissatisfied person
multi	faceted	multifaceted	having many sides or aspects
multi	form	multiform	having many different forms
phil	harmonic	philharmonic	fond of music (fil-har-*mon*-ik)

Prefixes Are Different Lengths

Prefixes can be as short as one letter or as long as six letters. The following chart shows some examples:

Number of Letters	Prefix	Sample Words	Meaning
One-Letter Prefix	a	amoral	not moral (ay-*mor*-al)
Two-Letter Prefix	co	cohabit	live together
Three-Letter Prefix	pre	premature	before mature
Four-Letter Prefix	para	paragraph	subsection of a writing
Five-Letter Prefix	tract	tractile	ductile; able to be drawn out
Six-Letter Prefix	circum	circumlocution	a roundabout way of speaking (sir-cum-loh-*que*-shun)

Prefixes Can Have More Than One Meaning

For example, the Latin prefix *in-* can mean "in" (as in inhabit), but it can also mean *not* (as in *inhuman*). As a result, knowing a prefix will take you only so far in defining testworthy words. You'll also have to use context clues to check meaning.

Here are some examples of Latin prefixes that have more than one meaning:

Prefix	Meaning	Examples
in	in, into	inhabit
in	not	inflexible
il	in, into	illuminate
il	not	illiterate
im	in, into	import
im	not	immodest
ir	in, into	irradiate
ir	not	irregular

Prefixes Can Have More Than One Spelling

For instance, the prefix for "together" can be spelled *syn-* or *sym-*. The prefix for "apart" can be spelled *dis-*, *di-*, and *dif-*. Ignore these minor variations because the prefix still has the same meaning.

Vocabulary Builder 1

Directions: There are fifteen words hidden in this word-find puzzle. Ten words have already been covered in this chapter, but five are new. To complete the puzzle, locate and circle all the words. The words may be written forward, backward, or upside down.

r	e	a	b	s	o	r	b	x	b	i	g	d	n
e	c	t	n	e	t	n	o	c	l	a	m	e	g
a	m	o	r	a	l	l	d	i	c	u	l	m	i
c	o	h	a	b	i	t	r	a	b	i	d	e	l
q	c	o	l	l	o	q	u	i	a	l	d	n	a
u	q	r	e	t	n	i	s	i	d	o	l	t	m
a	b	t	i	d	e	r	c	s	i	d	l	i	q
i	n	t	r	a	c	t	a	b	l	e	z	a	l
n	g	i	m	r	o	f	i	t	l	u	m	q	q
t	r	a	c	t	i	l	e	d	e	l	u	d	e

Vocabulary Builder 1 Answers

1. **multiform:** having many different forms
2. **cohabit:** live together
3. **intractable:** hard to handle; unmanageable
4. **disinter:** to unearth
5. **reacquaint:** meet again
6. **malcontent:** a dissatisfied person
7. **amoral:** not moral
8. **tractile:** ductile; able to be drawn out
9. **reabsorb:** absorb again
10. **discredit:** to cause to be doubted
11. **colloquial:** informal, as in conversation or writing
12. **lucid:** clear; bright
13. **delude:** to deceive
14. **malign:** to speak badly of another with the intent to harm
15. **dementia:** a loss of mental abilities or powers

LEARNING WORDS WITH GREEK PREFIXES

Ten Useful Greek Prefixes

As you learned in Chapter 5, many important TOEFL words have Greek roots. The same is true when it comes to Greek prefixes: many of the words that you encounter on standardized tests begin with Greek prefixes. Knowing these prefixes can help you decode and define many important words. Below are ten Greek prefixes that can help you do your best on the test.

Prefix	Meaning	Examples	Definition
a	not, without	atypical	not typical
		asymmetrical	not even
anthro	man	anthropology	study of man
		anthropoid	resembling man
anti	against	antipathy	hatred
		antisocial	unfriendly; misanthropic
aster/ astro	star	asteroid	star-like body (*as*-ter-oid)
		astrology	study of influence of stars on people
auto	self	autocracy	government by absolute monarch
		automate	operate without people
biblio	book	bibliophile	book lover (*bib*-lee-oh-file)
		bibliography	list of books (bib-lee-*ah*-graph-ee)
bio	life	biography	person's life story
		biofeedback	controlling bodily functions
chrom	color	chromophil	staining readily with dyes
		chromatics	the science of colors
chron	time	chronological	time order
		chronicle	history
cosmo	universe	cosmopolitan	worldly
		cosmonaut	a Russian astronaut

Vocabulary Builder 2

Directions: For each word, first write the prefix and its meaning. Then, use what you learned about prefixes to define each word. Feel free to look back at the ten prefixes you just learned.

Word	Prefix	Meaning	Word Meaning
1. anemia	_____	_____	_____
2. anthropoid	_____	_____	_____
3. antidote	_____	_____	_____
4. asterisk	_____	_____	_____
5. astronaut	_____	_____	_____
6. autonomous	_____	_____	_____
7. autonomy	_____	_____	_____
8. automation	_____	_____	_____
9. autopsy	_____	_____	_____
10. bibliophile	_____	_____	_____
11. biodegradable	_____	_____	_____
12. biopsy	_____	_____	_____
13. chronometer	_____	_____	_____
14. cosmos	_____	_____	_____
15. synchronize	_____	_____	_____

Vocabulary Builder 2 Answers

Word	Prefix	Meaning	Word Meaning
1. anemia	a	not	blood deficiency (uh-*nee*-me-uh)
2. anthropoid	anthro	man	resembling man
3. antidote	anti	against	remedy against poison
4. asterisk	aster	star	star-shaped mark
5. astronaut	astro	star	"star sailor"
6. autonomous	auto	self	self-governing
7. autonomy	auto	self	self-government
8. automation	auto	self	robot
9. autopsy	auto	self	inspection and dissection of a body after death
10. bibliophile	biblio	books	someone who values books
11. biodegradable	bio	life	decays and is absorbed into the environment
12. biopsy	bio	life	excision and study of a piece of bodily tissue
13. chronometer	chron	time	timepiece; watch
14. cosmos	cosmo	universe	universe
15. synchronize	chron	time	agree in time

Ten More Greek Prefixes

Below are ten more prefixes that have made their way from ancient Greece to modern English. Read through the prefixes, meanings, and examples. Pause after each row to see how many other words you can brainstorm that start with the same prefix.

Prefix	Meaning	Examples	Definition
dem	people	democracy	government by the people
eu	good	eulogize	speak well of someone (funeral speech) (*yoo*-low-gize)
gee, geo	earth	geography	writing about Earth
graph, gram	write	graphology	study of handwriting
hydro	water	hydrophobia	fear of water (hi-dro-*fo*-bee-uh)
hyper	over	hypercritical	overly critical
hypo	under	hypodermic	under the skin
micro	small	microscope	tool for looking at small objects
mis	hate	misanthropy	hatred of people (mis-*an*-throw-pee)
mono	one	monotone	one tone

Vocabulary Builder 3

Directions: First identify the prefix, then define it, and finally use what you learned to define the word. Refer to the previous chart if you need a quick review.

Word	Prefix	Meaning	Word Meaning
1. euphonious	_____	_____	_____
2. graphic	_____	_____	_____
3. microfilm	_____	_____	_____
4. apogee	_____	_____	_____
5. monotheism	_____	_____	_____
6. geology	_____	_____	_____
7. hydrology	_____	_____	_____
8. euphemism	_____	_____	_____
9. demagogue	_____	_____	_____
10. euphoria	_____	_____	_____

Vocabulary Builder 3 Answers

Word	Prefix	Meaning	Word Meaning
1. euphonious	eu	good	pleasing sound (you-*phone*-ee-us)
2. graphic	graph	write	written
3. microfilm	micro	small	small film
4. apogee	gee	earth	farthest point from Earth in satellite's orbit (*ah*-poe-gee)
5. monotheism	mono	one	one God
6. geology	geo	earth	study of the earth
7. hydrology	hydro	water	study of water (hi-*drah*-lo-gee)
8. euphemism	eu	good	substitution of a mild expression for one that may offend (*you*-fah-miz-um)
9. demagogue	dem	people	rabble-rouser
10. euphoria	eu	good	feeling of well-being (you-*for*-ee-uh)

Even More Greek Prefixes

Study the following ten additional Greek prefixes. As you read each one, look up and repeat the information to yourself. Then, write some of the least familiar words on note cards. Refer to these cards often to help you lock these testworthy words in your consciousness.

Prefix	Meaning	Examples	Definition
pan	all	panacea	cure-all
peri	around	perimeter	outer measurement
phil	love	philanthropy	love of humanity
phob	fear	phobia	fear
poly	many	polyphonic	many sounds
pseudo	false	pseudoscience	false science
psycho	mind	psychology	study of the mind
syn, sym	together	synthesis	putting together
tele	distance	telephone	phone
theo	God	theology	study of God or religion

Vocabulary Builder 4

Directions: Identify the prefix, define it, and then define the word. Feel free to look back at the chart if you need to refresh your memory. Remember: practice makes perfect.

Word	Prefix	Meaning	Word Meaning
1. synopsis	_____	_____	_____
2. telecommunication	_____	_____	_____
3. pandemic	_____	_____	_____
4. polynomial	_____	_____	_____
5. symmetrical	_____	_____	_____
6. Pan-American	_____	_____	_____
7. polyglot	_____	_____	_____
8. symbiosis	_____	_____	_____
9. telepathy	_____	_____	_____
10. polygon	_____	_____	_____

Vocabulary Builder 4 Answers

Word	Prefix	Meaning	Word Meaning
1. synopsis	syn	together	summary
2. telecommunication	tele	distance	communication across distances
3. pandemic	pan	all	widespread disease
4. polynomial	poly	many	a math expression having two or more terms
5. symmetrical	sym	together	identical parts
6. Pan-American	pan	all	all of the Americas
7. polyglot	poly	many	knowing many languages
8. symbiosis	sym	together	two dissimilar organisms living together off each other
9. telepathy	tele	distance	through transference
10. polygon	poly	many	figure with many sides

The Greek Prefix Arch-

An *architect* is a person who designs and oversees the construction of buildings. The Greeks called their architects *architektons*, or master builders. The word comes from the Greek prefix *archi* (chief) and the root *tekton* (workman).

The Greek prefix *arch* and the verb from which it is derived—*archein* (to be the first, to rule)—appear in many English words. The prefix is generally defined as "chief." The following chart shows some of these "arch" words that you are likely to find especially useful on the TOEFL.

Prefix	Example	Definition
arch	archbishop	chief of the church province
arch	archetype	original pattern or model (*ar*-keh-type)
arch	archaic	ancient (ar-*kay*-ic)
arch	archive	a place where public records are stored (*ar*-kive)
arch	archangel	chief angel

The Greek Prefix Cata-

Also from the Greeks comes the prefix *katarasso*, meaning "down rushing," as in rain or a river. Today, we use the word *cataract* to mean a waterfall or a deluge. As a medical term, a *cataract* is an opacity that blocks light from entering the lens of the eye. From these examples, it's clear that the word retains its sense of being a floodgate as well as a flood. The prefix *cata-* is defined as "down, against, or wholly."

Prefix	Example	Definition
cata	cataclysm	calamity (*cat*-uh-kliz-um)
cata	catalyst	reactant (*cat*-uh-list)
cata	catapult	throw, hurl (*cat*-uh-pult)
cata	catastrophe	disaster (cah-*tas*-stroh-fee)
cata	catacomb	underground passageways (*cat*-uh-kome)

LEARNING WORDS WITH LATIN PREFIXES

Latin has given us some extremely useful prefixes. The Latin prefix *circum* is a case in point. *Circum*, which means "around," can be used to form many useful everyday words. Here are twelve such examples:

The Latin Prefix Circum-

Word	Definition
circumjacent	surrounding
circumambulate	walk around
circumference	the outer boundary of something
circumfluent	flowing around
circumfuse	envelop
circumlocution	a roundabout way of speaking
circumnavigate	to sail around
circumpolar	around the North or South Pole
circumrotate	to rotate like a wheel
circumscribe	restrict
circumspect	cautious, prudent
circumvent	to get around

Ten Latin Prefixes

Study these ten Latin prefixes, their meanings, and examples.

Prefix	Meaning	Examples
a	to, toward	ascribe
act, ag	do, act	action
ad	to, toward	adverb
ante	before	anteroom
bene	good	beneficial
bi	two	bicycle
clud, clus	close	exclude inclusion
co, com	with, together	coworker, commotion
con, col	with, together	conduct, collaborate
contra	against, opposite	contraband
cur	run	current

Vocabulary Builder 5

> **Directions:** Time for fun! First unscramble each of the ten words so that it matches its definition. All but two of the words begin with prefixes. Then, use the words to fill the appropriate spaces on the corresponding line. When you have completed the entire puzzle, another word will read vertically in the column with circles.

1. elltaabrcoo   work together

2. seolobte   old-fashioned

3. vionec   beginner

4. yethpatle   communicating through transference

5. uqialyref   qualify again

6. oegape   farthest point from Earth in satellite's orbit

7. rnestdii   to unearth

8. aeactltrbin   hard to handle; unmanageable

9. ariidactntnoce   against indications

10. etyghool   study of God or religion

Vocabulary Builder 5 Answers

1. The correct answer is **collaborate**.

2. The correct answer is **obsolete**.

3. The correct answer is **novice**.

4. The correct answer is **telepathy**.

5. The correct answer is **requalify**.

6. The correct answer is **apogee**.

7. The correct answer is **disinter**.

8. The correct answer is **intractable**.

9. The correct answer is **contraindicate**.

10. The correct answer is **theology**.

Reading down: **contradict**.

Vocabulary Builder 6

Directions: Use what you've learned so far about Latin prefixes to figure out the meanings of the following ten words in boldface. Write the letter of your choice in the space provided.

_____ 1. cursive
(A) cruel
(B) commonplace
(C) criminal
(D) flowing handwriting

_____ 2. agitate
(A) clean
(B) tap your foot
(C) tranquilize
(D) stir up

_____ 3. adjoin
(A) separate
(B) listen closely
(C) touch
(D) disunite

_____ 4. cohabit
(A) nun's garb
(B) dependent
(C) change
(D) live together

_____ 5. concede
(A) yield
(B) build
(C) augment
(D) curtail

_____ **6.** depress
   (A) elevate
   (B) upraise
   (C) invigorate
   (D) bring down

_____ **7.** adjudicate
   (A) subjoin
   (B) deduct
   (C) lessen
   (D) arbitrate

_____ **8.** affix
   (A) withhold
   (B) repair
   (C) fasten
   (D) injure

_____ **9.** confederation
   (A) Southerners
   (B) antagonism
   (C) alliance
   (D) aversion

_____ **10.** collateral
   (A) security
   (B) far away
   (C) considerably
   (D) dependent

Vocabulary Builder 6 Answers

1. The correct answer is (D).

2. The correct answer is (D).

3. The correct answer is (C).

4. The correct answer is (D).

5. The correct answer is (A).

6. The correct answer is (D).

7. The correct answer is (D).

8. The correct answer is (C).

9. The correct answer is (C).

10. The correct answer is (A).

Ten More Testworthy Latin Prefixes

There are ten more Latin prefixes for you. Knowing just one prefix can help you figure out five or even more words. Consider how many words you can define when you know ten, twenty, or thirty prefixes!

Prefix	Meaning	Example	Definition
de	down	demolish	tear down
e	out	elongate	stretch out
ex	out	exchange	replace
inter	between	intercom	two-way radio
infra	under	infrared	rays under red
mal	bad	malodor	bad odor
male	evil	maledict	cursed
ob	toward	obedient	respectful
per	through	perambulate	walk through
post	after	postpone	do after

TIP

Remember: the more prefixes you learn, the more words you can decode.

Vocabulary Builder 7

Directions: Choose the best definition from the words in the box. You will have definitions left over.

flowing forth	teach	awkward
criminal	attractive	odd
vulgar	restless	comely
write on	dig out	invocation
compatriot	a fellow countryman	expedient
berate	compendium	pendant
to scold harshly	an abridged form of a work	principles
sound waves with a frequency below the audible range		

1. excavate _____

2. infrasonic _____

3. impart _____

4. maladroit _____

5. malefactor _____

6. eccentric _____

7. impatient _____

8. effluent _____

9. inscribe _____

10. indecent _____

Vocabulary Builder 7 Answers

1. The correct answer is **dig out.**

2. The correct answer is **sound waves with a frequency below the audible range.**

3. The correct answer is **teach.**

4. The correct answer is **awkward.**

5. The correct answer is **criminal.**

6. The correct answer is **odd.**

7. The correct answer is **restless.**

8. The correct answer is **flowing forth.**

9. The correct answer is **write on.**

10. The correct answer is **vulgar.**

PREFIXES FOR NUMBERS

The symbols we use for numbers—1, 2, 3, 4, etc.—come from the Arabs, the first great mathematicians. The words we use to speak or write these symbols—one, two, three, four, etc.—are from the Anglo-Saxons.

How many sides does the Pentagon have? How many tentacles does an octopus have? If you know your number prefixes, these questions are a snap to answer. The envelope, please: The _Pentagon_ has <u>five</u> sides (penta = five). An _octopus_ has <u>eight</u> tentacles (octo = eight).

As you can see, when we want to combine a number and a word to form another word, such as a synonym for a "five-sided figure," we use the Greek or Roman word for the number, pentameter.

Below are ten Greek and Latin prefixes that show the numbers one to ten.

Number	Prefix	Example	Definition
1	uni	unicycle	cycle with one wheel
2	bi	bicycle	cycle with two wheels
3	tri	tripod	three-legged stand
4	quad	quadrangle	four-sided figure
5	penta	pentameter	five-sided figure
6	hexa	hexagon	six-sided figure
7	hepta	Heptateuch	the first seven books of the Hebrew Bible
8	oct	octet	a group of eight, usually singers (ock-_tet_)
9	nov	novena	Roman Catholic prayers or services conducted on nine consecutive days
10	deca	decathlon	ten-event athletic contest (di-_kath_-lon)

ANGLO-SAXON PREFIXES

Below are the five most common Anglo-Saxon prefixes and their variations. Read through the chart and examples. To help you remember the prefixes, complete the self-test that follows.

Prefix	Meaning	Examples	Definition
a	on, to, at, by	ablaze	on fire
be	around, over	besiege	attack
mis	wrong, badly	mistake	error
over	above, beyond	overreach	reach too high
un	not	unambiguous	clear (un-am-_big_-yoo-us)

Vocabulary Builder 8

Directions: Based on the meaning of its prefix, define each of the following words:

1. accord _____

2. irradiate _____

3. predestination _____

4. reincarnation _____

5. convolute _____

6. invoke _____

7. irrelevant _____

8. excommunicate _____

Vocabulary Builder 8 Answers

1.   The correct answer is **agreement.**

2.   The correct answer is **illuminate.**

3.   The correct answer is **fate.**

4.   The correct answer is **rebirth.**

5.   The correct answer is **twist up.**

6.   The correct answer is **request.**

7.   The correct answer is **not pertinent.**

8.   The correct answer is **exclude from communion.**

EXERCISES: WORDS IN CONTEXT

Directions: Define each of the following underlined words, based on the way it is used in the phrase. Write the letter of your choice in the space provided.

_____1. miscarriage of justice
  (A) benediction
  (B) detail
  (C) villain
  (D) failure

_____2. beseech emotionally
  (A) implore
  (B) deny
  (C) shriek
  (D) pursue

_____3. something strange is afoot
  (A) underneath
  (B) going on
  (C) clandestine
  (D) covert

_____4. unethical behavior
  (A) judicial
  (B) impartial
  (C) unprincipled
  (D) competent

_____5. an overwrought child
  (A) heavy
  (B) unmannerly
  (C) placid
  (D) excited

exercises

EXERCISES: PREFIXES

> **Directions:** Each of the following words starts with a prefix. Use what you learned about prefixes to see how many of these words you can define. Select the correct meaning for each of the following boldfaced words. Circle your choice.

1. **accede**
   go very fast
   agree
   excessive
   debate

2. **hypocrisy**
   overpriced
   false virtue
   sweet natured
   injection

3. **subsistence**
   wealth
   existing
   under water
   farming

4. **aggregate**
   complete
   annoy
   marbles
   clot

5. **ultramarine**
   fashionable
   weird
   deep blue
   famous

6. **hyperactivity**
   illness
   medicine
   excessive activity
   slow

7. **catacomb**
   comb for cats
   dessert
   underground room
   crooked

8. **amoral**
   very moral
   not moral
   story lesson
   high spirits

9. **compress**
   squeeze
   heal
   measurement tool
   pat

10. **supercilious**
    arrogant
    high achieving
    very silly
    long hairs

EXERCISES: SYNONYMS

Directions: Circle the answer choice that is the synonym for the underlined word.

1. He was <u>inflexible</u> in his determination to unite his country.

   (A) inflatable

   (B) infernal

   (C) infantile

   (D) inexorable

2. By the time peace was negotiated, the affairs of the nation were in a <u>chaotic</u> state.

   (A) confused

   (B) exotic

   (C) disputable

   (D) obscure

3. Because the author and the artist refused to <u>collaborate</u>, the book was never finished.

   (A) confide

   (B) collate

   (C) provide proof

   (D) work together

4. After World War II, the Vietnamese believed that the French would allow them to be an <u>autonomous</u> people.

   (A) self-respecting

   (B) self-governing

   (C) self-reliant

   (D) self-supporting

5. He took a <u>militant</u> stand against the opposition and won the point.

   (A) mild

   (B) aggressive

   (C) positive

   (D) awkward

6. The Communist <u>regime</u> favored unification of the country.

   (A) leader

   (B) government

   (C) regiment

   (D) register

7. The North Vietnamese gained <u>ascendancy</u> over the south after many years of warfare.

   (A) defeat

   (B) rising

   (C) ascription

   (D) power

EXERCISES: PUTTING IT TOGETHER

Directions: Now, do this crossword puzzle to review some of the vocabulary you have practiced.

<table>
<tr><td>

Across

1. Yield
6. Eager
8. Angry
12. Piece of land, as in parking _____
13. Preposition: _____ the same time
14. Negative word
15. Prefix meaning *against*
16. Unmoving
17. Inter
19. Have you _____ Tom?
20. Cause
23. Very valuable object
25. Ability

</td><td>

Down

1. Unfeeling
2. Harmful
3. Abbreviation for *kitchen*
4. Abbreviation for *street*
5. Quality, characteristic
6. Equipment
7. Poison
8. Wounds
9. Careless and impolite
10. Prefix meaning *before*
11. Antonym of *yes*
15. Entrance, means of reaching
18. Neither/_____

</td></tr>
</table>

Across

26. Use the eyes
28. Informal word for *friend*
29. Conclave
31. What is expected, usual, or average
33. Scold, rebuke
36. Wrong, faulty
39. Abbreviation for *North America*
40. Suffix used to form a noun from *occur*
41. Atmosphere
42. An infant is totally _____ upon its mother.

Down

20. Subject pronoun
21. Has the sun always _____
22. Vigor
24. Clear and definite
25. Soothe, relieve
27. Circum, peri
30. Conjunction
32. Prefix meaning *two*
34. Uni, mono
35. Feminine pronoun
36. Indefinite article
37. Abbreviation for *medium*
38. Abbreviation for *separate*

exercises

ANSWER KEY

Words in Context

1.	D	4.	C
2.	A	5.	D
3.	B		

Prefixes

1.	agree	6.	excessive activity
2.	false virtue	7.	underground room
3.	existing	8.	not moral
4.	complete	9.	squeeze
5.	deep blue	10.	arrogant

Synonyms

1.	D	5.	B
2.	A	6.	B
3.	D	7.	D
4.	B		

Putting It Together

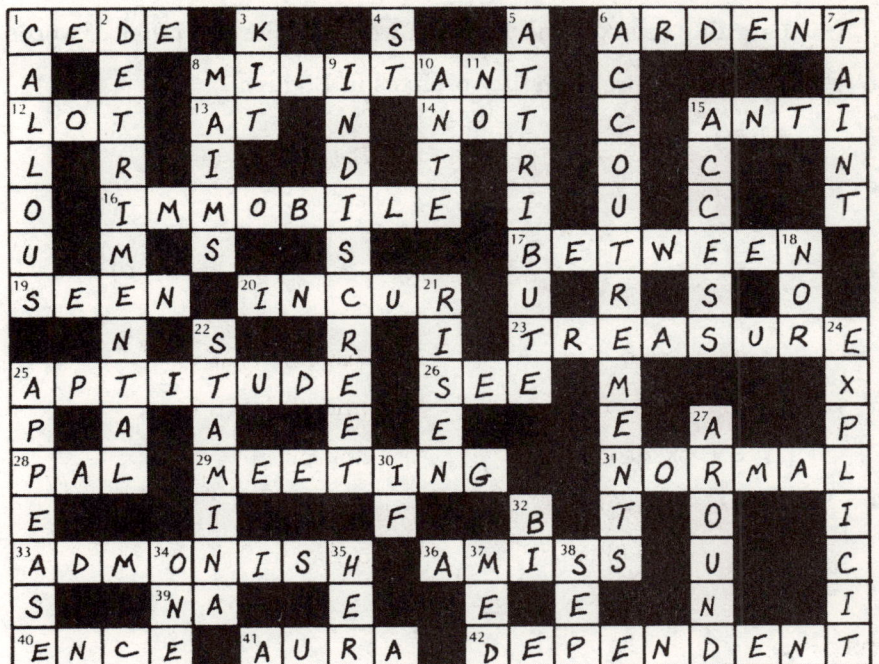

SUMMING IT UP

- Learning prefixes will help you work out the meanings of words.

- There are more than fifty prefixes in English.

All About Suffixes

OVERVIEW

- **Suffixes**
- **Strategies for learning suffixes**
- **How suffixes work**
- **Suffixes that describe state of being**
- **Suffixes that indicate occupations**
- **Suffixes that show resemblance**
- **Suffixes that show amount**
- **Twelve useful suffixes**
- **Summing it up**

SUFFIXES

A **suffix** is a combination of letters added to the end of a word or word root. Suffixes are used either to form new words or show the function of a word. For example, the suffix *-ist* or *-ian* added to a noun describes people, forming words like "motorist" and "musician."

In this chapter, you will learn some common suffixes that identify nouns, verbs, adjectives, and adverbs to help you recognize errors in word forms. You can also improve your vocabulary as you learn how these common suffixes change words from one part of speech to another.

STRATEGIES FOR LEARNING SUFFIXES

Remember that suffixes or word forms are the most common type of error tested on the TOEFL.

- Check for word form errors that include the use of words related to certain fields and the people who work in the field (botany, botanical, a botanist).
- Check for word form errors involving adjectives and nouns (developing/ development).
- Check for other word form errors, such as a noun in place of a verb (belief/ believe).

chapter 7

HOW SUFFIXES WORK

Suffixes Are Added to the End of Roots to Create Many Words

In the same way that prefixes are placed at the beginning of a word to change its meaning, suffixes are placed at the *end* to change a word's meaning. Here are some examples:

Word +	Suffix =	Word	Definition
allege	ation	allegation	assertion, claim
recognize	tion	recognition	identification
alien	ation	alienation	estrangement, cut off from
peril	ous	perilous	dangerous
hazard	ous	hazardous	dangerous
capacity	ous	capacious	large, roomy
tonsils	itis	tonsillitis	inflammation of the tonsils
bronchi	itis	bronchitis	inflammation of the lung region
appendix	itis	appendicitis	inflammation of the appendix

Suffixes Are Always Attached to Words Without a Break

Even though you may have seen the suffix written with a hyphen (as in *-eous*, *-ion*, *-ment*), the suffix is attached without a hyphen. The following chart shows some examples:

Word +	Suffix =	New Word	Definition
combust	ible	combustible	flammable
pasture	al	pastoral	country-like
palace	ial	palatial	like a palace
abstain	ious	abstemious	moderate, sober
wasp	ish	waspish	irritable, crabby
fellow	ship	fellowship	sociability

Suffixes Are Different Lengths

As with prefixes, suffixes can be as short as one letter or far longer. The following chart shows some examples:

Number of Letters	Suffix	Word	Pronunciation	Meaning
One-Letter Suffix	d	promulgated	(*prom*-mul-gay-ted)	to publish or disseminate widely
Two-Letter Suffix	ed	besmirched	(bee-*smirchd*)	to soil; make filthy
Three-Letter Suffix	ity	instability		not stable
Four-Letter Suffix	ment	inducement	(in-*doos*-ment)	incentive
Five-Letter Suffix	ation	vacillation	(vah-ci-*lay*-shun)	indecision

Suffixes Can Affect How a Word Functions in a Sentence

Unlike prefixes, suffixes can create a part of speech. For example, adding a suffix can change a word from a verb to an adjective, as in *risk* to *risky*.

Adjective
The following suffixes show that a word is an *adjective* (word that describes):

-ful   -less   -able/-ible   -y

Noun
The following suffixes show that a word is a *noun* (person, place, or thing):

-ance/-ence   -ful   -ment   -sion/-tion   -age   -ity

Verb
The following suffixes show that a word is a *verb* (action or state of being):

-ate   -en   -ite   -ize

If you know a word's part of speech, you can figure out how it is being used—even if you don't know its meaning. Study the following examples:

Word	Suffix	Part of Speech	Meaning
bountiful	-ful	adjective	plentiful
boundless	-less	adjective	infinite
perdurable	-able	adjective	permanent; everlasting
frangible	-ible	adjective	easily broken
fallible	-ible	adjective	makes mistakes
decadence	-ence	noun	deterioration, esp. in morality
mouthful	-ful	noun	morsel
excrement	-ment	noun	matter expelled or ejected; waste
perdition	-tion	noun	entire loss; utter destruction; ruin
premonition	-tion	noun	a forewarning
posterity	-ity	noun	those who come after
abdicate	-ate	verb	to formally relinquish or renounce an office or right
mutate	-ate	verb	change
extradite	-ite	verb	to deliver (give up) a criminal from one state or nation to another
demonize	-ize	verb	make a demon

TIP

Whenever you come upon an unfamiliar word, first check to see if it has a recognizable root.

Suffixes Can Change a Word's Tense (or Time)

For instance, adding -d or -ed makes a present-tense verb into a past-tense verb, as the following chart shows:

Present tense	Past tense	Meaning
denude	denuded	to strip bare
depose	deposed	to remove from a position
exacerbate	exacerbated	to make worse
expunge	expunged	to rub out; obliterate
embalm	embalmed	to inject a preservative into a corpse
embark	embarked	to board a ship or train for a trip
embellish	embellished	to decorate or make beautiful
envelop	enveloped	to assimilate (bring in as part of)
extradite	extradited	to give up a criminal from one state or nation to another
extrapolate	extrapolated	to deduce an unknown from a known

Adding a Suffix to the End of a Word Changes the Word's Meaning

For example: *kitchen* becomes *kitchenette*, the diminutive

Just as knowing a small number of prefixes and roots can help you figure out many unfamiliar words, so knowing a few everyday suffixes can help you decode many testworthy words.

Vocabulary Builder 1

Directions: There are fifteen words hidden in this word-find puzzle. Some of the words have already been covered in this chapter, but others are new. To complete the puzzle, locate and circle all the words. The words may be written forward, backward, or upside down.

```
c  a  t  a  r  a  c  t  e  d  u  n  e  d  m  a
a  l  l  e  g  a  t  i  o  n  n  o  w  s  i  d
p  c  n  o  i  t  a  l  l  i  c  a  v  x  s  e
a  b  s  t  e  m  i  o  u  s  b  i  g  x  n  g
c  a  b  b  e  s  m  i  r  c  h  e  d  m  o  n
i  z  z  d  e  t  a  g  l  u  m  o  r  p  m  u
o  q  u  e  p  i  t  h  e  t  w  i  g  e  e  p
u  z  e  x  a  c  e  r  b  a  t  e  d  q  r  x
s  x  d  e  t  i  d  a  r  t  x  e  a  a  a  e
e  h  s  i  l  l  e  b  m  e  p  r  o  l  i  x
```

Vocabulary Builder 1 Answers

1. **capacious:** large, roomy

2. **cataract:** a waterfall

3. **epithet:** a word or phrase describing a person; a derogatory word or phrase used to show contempt

4. **besmirched:** to soil; make filthy

5. **exacerbated:** to make worse

6. **denude:** to strip bare

7. **misnomer:** a wrong name or designation

8. **embellish:** to decorate or make beautiful

9. **prolix:** needlessly prolonged or drawn out

10. **expunged:** to rub out; obliterate

11. **extradited:** to give up a criminal from one state or nation to another

12. **vacillation:** indecision

13. **promulgated:** publish or disseminate widely

14. **abstemious:** moderate, sober

15. **allegation:** assertion, claim

SUFFIXES THAT DESCRIBE STATE OF BEING

Below are twelve suffixes that describe a state of being. How many more words can you think of that end with these suffixes that describe a state of being?

Suffix	Example
-ance	appearance
-ant	deviant
-cy	infancy
-dom	freedom
-ence	independence
-ent	corpulent
-hood	neighborhood
-mony	matrimony
-ness	lightness
-sis	thesis
-tic	gigantic
-ty	novelty

Vocabulary Builder 2

Directions: For each word, first write the suffix and its meaning. Then, use what you've learned about suffixes to define each word. Don't hesitate to look back at what you just learned or to use a dictionary if you would like to.

Word	Suffix	Suffix Meaning	Word Meaning
1. goodness	_____	_____	_____
2. anxiety	_____	_____	_____
3. brilliance	_____	_____	_____
4. despondence	_____	_____	_____
5. catharsis	_____	_____	_____
6. effulgent	_____	_____	_____
7. hypothesis	_____	_____	_____
8. resilient	_____	_____	_____

Word	Suffix	Suffix Meaning	Word Meaning
9. repellent	_____	_____	_____
10. officialdom	_____	_____	_____
11. thrifty	_____	_____	_____
12. bibliomancy	_____	_____	_____
13. truculent	_____	_____	_____
14. brotherhood	_____	_____	_____
15. convalescence	_____	_____	_____
16. adamant	_____	_____	_____
17. diligent	_____	_____	_____
18. parity	_____	_____	_____
19. disenchant	_____	_____	_____
20. ambivalent	_____	_____	_____

Vocabulary Builder 2 Answers

Word	Suffix	Meaning	Word Meaning
1. goodness	-ness	state of being	being good
2. anxiety	-ty	state of being	nervousness
3. brilliance	-ance	state of being	brightness
4. despondence	-ence	state of being	sadness
5. catharsis	-sis	state of being	purging
6. effulgent	-ent	state of being	flowing
7. hypothesis	-sis	state of being	guess
8. resilient	-ent	state of being	elastic
9. repellent	-ent	state of being	offensive
10. officialdom	-dom	state of being	authoritative
11. thrifty	-ty	state of being	frugal
12. bibliomancy	-cy	state of being	Biblical books
13. truculent	-ent	state of being	harsh
14. brotherhood	-hood	state of being	friendship
15. convalescence	-ence	state of being	recovering
16. adamant	-ant	state of being	definite
17. diligent	-ent	state of being	hard-working
18. parity	-ty	state of being	equality
19. disenchant	-ant	state of being	disillusion
20. ambivalent	-ent	state of being	unsure

SUFFIXES THAT INDICATE OCCUPATIONS

A *lawyer* is someone who deals with the law; a *buyer* is someone who buys items. Below are ten suffixes that indicate a person who is something, does something, or deals with something.

Suffix	Example
-ar	scholar
-ard	dullard
-ary	revolutionary
-er	conjurer (magician)
-ian	historian
-ier	furrier
-ist	psychologist
-ite	socialite
-or	bettor

The Suffix *-ist*

Many useful words have been formed with the suffix "*ist*." Often, these words describe hobbies or careers. The following chart shows the most testworthy of these words:

Word	Definition	Pronunciation
aborist	deals with tree care	*ahr*-bur-ist
entomologist	deals with insects	en-tuh-*mahl*-uh-jist
geneticist	deals with heredity	juh-*net*-uh-sist
meteorologist	deals with the weather	meet-ee-uh-*ral*-uh-jist
numismatist	deals with coins	noo-*miz*-muh-tist
philatelist	deals with stamps	fuh-*lat*-uh-list
psychologist	deals with people's problems	sy-*kahl*-uh-jist

Vocabulary Builder 3

Directions: Match the word to its definition. If you wish, underline the suffix in each word to help you remember how they are used. Write your answers in the space provided.

_____	1. functionary	**a.**	philosopher, scholar
_____	2. editor	**b.**	person who sits
_____	3. taxidermist	**c.**	person who edits
_____	4. comedian	**d.**	mediator
_____	5. arbitrator	**e.**	an official
_____	6. pedestrian	**f.**	opponent
_____	7. theorist	**g.**	handwriting
_____	8. adversary	**h.**	person who stuffs animals
_____	9. sedentary	**i.**	person who walks
_____	10. penmanship	**j.**	humorist

Vocabulary Builder 3 Answers

1. The correct answer is e.
2. The correct answer is c.
3. The correct answer is h.
4. The correct answer is j.
5. The correct answer is d.
6. The correct answer is i.
7. The correct answer is a.
8. The correct answer is f.
9. The correct answer is b.
10. The correct answer is g.

SUFFIXES THAT SHOW RESEMBLANCE

Below are twelve suffixes that all mean "resembling, like, or of." Study them and the examples. Then, complete the activity that follows to help you incorporate these words and suffixes into your daily vocabulary.

Suffix	Example	Definition
-ac	cardiac	having to do with the heart
-al	natural	having to do with nature
-an	suburban	having to do with the suburbs
-esque	statuesque	curvaceous, shapely
-ile	infantile	like a child
-ine	masculine	manly
-ish	foolish	asinine
-ly	yearly	occurring every year
-ory	advisory	helping out
-oid	android	human-like
-some	worrisome	distressing, disconcerting
-wise	likewise	in the same way

Vocabulary Builder 4

Directions: In the space provided, write **T** if the definition is true and **F** if it is false. Use what you learned about suffixes that mean "resembling, like, or of" to help you figure out what each word means.

_____ 1. devilish   like a devil

_____ 2. cuboid   like a cube

_____ 3. puerile   mature

_____ 4. saturnine   sluggish, gloomy

_____ 5. fulsome   shortage

_____ 6. sensory   pertaining to the senses

_____ 7. Romanesque   like the Romans

_____ 8. pastoral   wild, untamed

_____ 9. ovoid   like an egg

_____ 10. dollarwise   pertaining to money

_____ 11. fictional   factual

_____ 12. churlish   polite

Vocabulary Builder 4 Answers

1. The correct answer is T.

2. The correct answer is T.

3. The correct answer is F.

4. The correct answer is T.

5. The correct answer is F.

6. The correct answer is T.

7. The correct answer is F.

8. The correct answer is F.

9. The correct answer is T.

10. The correct answer is T.

11. The correct answer is F.

12. The correct answer is F.

Vocabulary Builder 5

Directions: Each of the following boldfaced words ends with a suffix. Use what you already know about suffixes to see how many of these words you can decode. Select the correct meaning and write the letter of your choice in the space provided.

_____1. culinary

   (A) cute; attractive

   (B) picky

   (C) dealing with cooking

   (D) dealing with cue balls

_____2. insignificance

   (A) momentous

   (B) sign; insignia

   (C) consequential

   (D) unimportant

_____3. palatial

   (A) luxurious

   (B) incomplete

   (C) roof of the mouth

   (D) paradigm

_____4. seditious

   (A) rebellious

   (B) cooperative

   (C) mutual

   (D) perspicacious

_____5. intransigent

   (A) not traveling

   (B) insolvent

   (C) close-minded

   (D) prolific

_____6. erudite

   (A) ruddy-skinned

   (B) pencil lead

   (C) synergistic

   (D) learned

_____7. apothecary
- (A) pharmacist
- (B) quack
- (C) heavy burden
- (D) demagogue

_____8. partisan
- (A) windmill
- (B) section
- (C) supporter
- (D) cadaver

_____9. preponderance
- (A) minority
- (B) immaturity
- (C) overweight
- (D) majority

_____10. mercenary
- (A) generous
- (B) avaricious
- (C) docile
- (D) dogmatic

Vocabulary Builder 5 Answers

1. The correct answer is (C).

2. The correct answer is (D).

3. The correct answer is (A).

4. The correct answer is (A).

5. The correct answer is (C).

6. The correct answer is (D).

7. The correct answer is (A).

8. The correct answer is (C).

9. The correct answer is (D).

10. The correct answer is (B).

SUFFIXES THAT SHOW AMOUNT

Below are ten suffixes that show quantity. Some of these suffixes were discussed earlier in this chapter in a different context. This was done on purpose because repetition makes it easier for you to remember crucial testworthy words and concepts.

Suffix	Meaning	Example	Pronunciation	Definition
-aceous	having	curvaceous	cur-*vay*-shush	having curves
-ed	characterized by	cultured	*kul*-churd	civilized
-lent	inclined to be	prevalent	*preh*-vah-lent	common
-ose	full of	morose	more-*ose*	gloomy
-ous	full of	perilous	*per*-ih-lus	dangerous
-ious	having	vicious	*vish*-us	vile
-less	without	guiltless		innocent
-ling	minor	yearling		year-old horse
-fold	increased by	tenfold		ten times
-ful	full	healthful		nutritious

TWELVE USEFUL SUFFIXES

Let's finish up with some important suffixes that crop up in many of the words you will encounter in your academic career.

Suffix	Meaning	Example	Pronunciation	Definition
-erly	to, directly	easterly	*ees*-ter-lee	go east
-escent	beginning	opalescent	oh-pah-*less*-ent	shiny
-eum	place for	museum		storehouse of exhibits
-ferous	carrying, bearing	odoriferous	oh-dur-*if*-ur-us	stinky
-ia	condition	anorexia	an-uh-*reks*-ee-uh	eating disorder
-fy	marked by	magnify		make larger
-ical	having to do with	musical		lyric
-id	inclined to be	florid	*flor*-id	gaudy
-ive	inclined to be	festive	*fes*-tive	joyful
-ism	practice/quality	baptism	*bap*-tiz-um	religious ceremony
-tude	condition	rectitude	*rek*-tuh-tood	virtue
-ure	means, quality	rapture	*rap*-chur	bliss

Vocabulary Builder 6

> **Directions:** Match each word in the first column to its definition in the second column. If you wish, underline the suffix in each word to help you remember how it is used. Write your answers in the space provided.

_____ 1.	bursitis	**a.**	eager
_____ 2.	discernment	**b.**	to suggest
_____ 3.	nihilism	**c.**	surrender
_____ 4.	adolescence	**d.**	inflammation of the bursa (area between the bone and a tendon)
_____ 5.	expenditure	**e.**	open-air theater
_____ 6.	abandonment	**f.**	judgment
_____ 7.	heroism	**g.**	reversion; throwback
_____ 8.	inducement	**h.**	enhance
_____ 9.	intensify	**i.**	expenses
_____ 10.	signify	**j.**	bravery
_____ 11.	coliseum	**k.**	teen years
_____ 12.	obsolescent	**l.**	used up
_____ 13.	fervid	**m.**	repudiation
_____ 14.	sinusitis	**n.**	inflammation of sinuses
_____ 15.	atavism	**o.**	motive

Vocabulary Builder 6 Answers

1. The correct answer is d.
2. The correct answer is f.
3. The correct answer is m.
4. The correct answer is k.
5. The correct answer is i.
6. The correct answer is c.
7. The correct answer is j.
8. The correct answer is o.
9. The correct answer is h.
10. The correct answer is b.

11. **The correct answer is e.**

12. **The correct answer is l.**

13. **The correct answer is a.**

14. **The correct answer is n.**

15. **The correct answer is g.**

Vocabulary Builder 7

Directions: Select the correct meaning for each of the following boldfaced words. Use what you learned about suffixes as well as all the other vocabulary techniques you have mastered so far. Circle your answer choice.

1. The murder scene can only be described as a **carnage**.

    (A) confusion

    (B) cluttered area

    (C) holy area

    (D) massacre

2. The drunk's **clownish** actions embarrassed his family.

    (A) amusing

    (B) admirable

    (C) foolish

    (D) humorous

3. The lawyer functioned as an **intermediary** between the warring couple.

    (A) junta

    (B) friend

    (C) confidant

    (D) mediator

4. Some people think that acne is **chromosomal**.

    (A) genetic

    (B) judicious

    (C) conjugal

    (D) abnormal

5. The new college president kicked off his appointment with a big **convocation**.

    (A) speech

    (B) gathering

    (C) rejoinder

    (D) lexicon

6. The preacher had an annoying habit of **proselytizing** at inappropriate moments.
    - **(A)** eating
    - **(B)** attempting to convert people to his way of thinking
    - **(C)** trying to sleep
    - **(D)** elucidating

7. Children hate to be **castigated** in front of their friends.
    - **(A)** praised
    - **(B)** rebuked
    - **(C)** out in a cast
    - **(D)** mercurial

8. There was no doubt who was **culpable** for the mistake.
    - **(A)** able to cope
    - **(B)** out of control
    - **(C)** impenitent
    - **(D)** liable

9. The florist placed flowers, moss, and stones in the **terrarium**.
    - **(A)** a shallow pool
    - **(B)** case
    - **(C)** an environment for plants and land animals
    - **(D)** an environment for extinct creatures

10. After treatment, the former alcoholic was happy to be **abstinent**.
    - **(A)** conical
    - **(B)** stubborn
    - **(C)** intoxicated
    - **(D)** sober

Vocabulary Builder 7 Answers

1. The correct answer is (D).
2. The correct answer is (C).
3. The correct answer is (D).
4. The correct answer is (A).
5. The correct answer is (B).
6. The correct answer is (B).
7. The correct answer is (B).
8. The correct answer is (D).
9. The correct answer is (C).
10. The correct answer is (D).

EXERCISES: PREFIXES AND SUFFIXES

Directions: Find a word in this chapter that uses either the prefix or suffix given and write it on the first line. Then try to think of another word with the same prefix or suffix. Make sure you understand the meaning of all of the words that you write. If you don't, look them up in your dictionary.

1. -less:
   (A) _____
   (B) _____

2. -ers:
   (A) _____
   (B) _____

3. anti-:
   (A) _____
   (B) _____

4. -ful:
   (A) _____
   (B) _____

5. over-:
   (A) _____
   (B) _____

6. hyper-:
   (A) _____
   (B) _____

7. ex-:
   (A) _____
   (B) _____

8. -ious:
   (A) _____
   (B) _____

Directions: Choose the best answer.

9. The prefix *pro* in the word *proponent* means
   (A) professional
   (B) property
   (C) against
   (D) for

10. The prefix in *redefining* means
   (A) clearly
   (B) later
   (C) informally
   (D) again

11. The suffix *ist* in *environmentalist* and *ecologist* indicates
   (A) an area
   (B) a thing
   (C) a person
   (D) a time

12. The prefix *fore* in *foresee* means
   (A) at the same time
   (B) before
   (C) in favor of
   (D) beside

EXERCISES: SYNONYMS

Directions: Circle the answer choice that has the same meaning as the underlined word.

1. A gun is a <u>lethal</u> weapon.
   (A) dangerous
   (B) modern
   (C) deadly
   (D) light

2. A soothsayer can <u>foresee</u> events.
   (A) see after
   (B) see behind
   (C) see before
   (D) see now

3. In order to save a ship in a storm, in the old days the crew <u>jettisoned</u> the cargo.
   (A) loaded
   (B) ate
   (C) threw overboard
   (D) tied down

4. Constant <u>wrangles</u> over money disturbed the harmony of their marriage.
   (A) discussions
   (B) problems
   (C) bills
   (D) arguments

5. Many civilians were <u>maimed</u> in the air raid.
   (A) killed
   (B) wounded
   (C) evacuated
   (D) molested

6. The beaver dam <u>obstructed</u> the flow of the river.
   (A) observed
   (B) endangered
   (C) assisted
   (D) blocked off

7. <u>Toxic</u> waste disposal is a major concern at a nuclear power plant.
   (A) poisonous
   (B) superfluous
   (C) metallic
   (D) liquid

8. The neighbors' swimming pool <u>infringed</u> upon my property.
   (A) remained
   (B) threatened
   (C) implicated
   (D) encroached

9. Following the <u>fiasco</u> at the nuclear plant, the public protested its reopening.
   (A) partial breakdown
   (B) complete failure
   (C) boycott
   (D) destructive fire

10. The negotiations reached an <u>impasse</u> because the union representatives walked out of the meeting.
    (A) solution
    (B) impossibility
    (C) rejection
    (D) deadlock

11. The Red Cross arrived at the <u>disaster</u> area within 24 hours.

    (A) calamity

    (B) destruction

    (C) departure

    (D) hurricane

12. The earthquake caused great <u>devastation</u> in California.

    (A) ruin

    (B) confusion

    (C) movement

    (D) gaps

13. Nestor's <u>sage</u> suggestions saved the Greeks from calamity.

    (A) repeated

    (B) wise

    (C) helpful

    (D) ingenious

14. <u>Proponents</u> of conservation oppose the new laws.

    (A) antagonists

    (B) properties

    (C) advocates

    (D) proposals

15. The President's former supporters have <u>repudiated</u> his current economic plan.

    (A) rejected

    (B) supported

    (C) hailed

    (D) divorced

exercises

EXERCISES: PUTTING IT TOGETHER

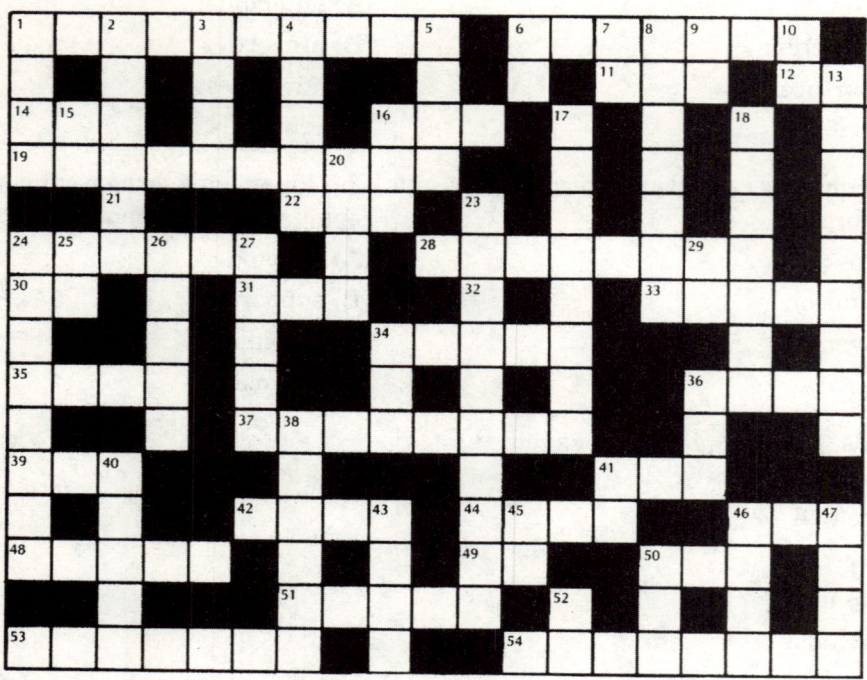

Across

1. Careful; honest
6. Inactive
11. Consume
12. Preposition: _____ the table
14. Vacant space
16. Prefix meaning *wrong*
19. Rudimentary
21. Indefinite article
22. Abbreviation for *streets*
24. Existing but not yet active
28. Encroach
30. Preposition: _____ home
31. Masculine pronoun
32. Prefix meaning *out*
33. Where are you _____?
34. Poisonous
35. First word of letter salutation

Down

1. Wise
2. Do again
3. You're very _____; are you sick?
4. Names of things written to keep them in order
5. Remain
6. Auxiliary verb
7. Prefix meaning *again*
8. Wounding
9. See 30 Across
10. Antonym of *from*
13. Careless
15. Suffix used to change *arrive* to a noun
16. Title for a married woman
17. Draws toward
18. Antonym of *give*

Across

36. Past participle of *be*

37. Fights, argues

39. Container used to carry groceries

41. Superlative ending

42. Eager, enthusiastic

44. Convince

46. Money charged for a service

48. Period of time

49. Conjunction

50. United States of America

51. Incalculable

53. Soothe, relieve

54. Very close, next to

Down

20. Type of bomb

23. Unclear, vague

24. Deserving praise

25. See 9 Down

26. Prefix meaning *beyond*

27. Antonym of *catch*

29. Antonym of *come*

34. Number of events in a decathlon

36. However

38. Destroy

40. Number of people or things put together

41. Prefix meaning *out*

43. Legal document

45. Preposition in 50 Across

46. Succeed

47. Way out

50. See 50 Across

52. Advertisement

ANSWER KEY

Prefixes and Suffixes

1–8. Answers will vary

9. D

10. D

11. C

12. B

Synonyms

1.	C	6.	D	11.	A
2.	C	7.	A	12.	A
3.	C	8.	D	13.	B
4.	D	9.	B	14.	C
5.	B	10.	D	15.	A

Putting It Together

SUMMING IT UP

- Suffixes are added to the ends of roots to create many words.

- Suffixes are of different lengths.

- Adding a suffix to the end of a word can change its meaning or its tense.

PART IV

TWO PRACTICE TESTS

Practice Test 2

Practice Test 3

ANSWER SHEET PRACTICE TEST 2

1. Ⓐ Ⓑ Ⓒ Ⓓ   11. Ⓐ Ⓑ Ⓒ Ⓓ   21. Ⓐ Ⓑ Ⓒ Ⓓ   31. Ⓐ Ⓑ Ⓒ Ⓓ   41. Ⓐ Ⓑ Ⓒ Ⓓ

2. Ⓐ Ⓑ Ⓒ Ⓓ   12. Ⓐ Ⓑ Ⓒ Ⓓ   22. Ⓐ Ⓑ Ⓒ Ⓓ   32. Ⓐ Ⓑ Ⓒ Ⓓ   42. Ⓐ Ⓑ Ⓒ Ⓓ

3. Ⓐ Ⓑ Ⓒ Ⓓ   13. Ⓐ Ⓑ Ⓒ Ⓓ   23. Ⓐ Ⓑ Ⓒ Ⓓ   33. Ⓐ Ⓑ Ⓒ Ⓓ   43. Ⓐ Ⓑ Ⓒ Ⓓ

4. Ⓐ Ⓑ Ⓒ Ⓓ   14. Ⓐ Ⓑ Ⓒ Ⓓ   24. Ⓐ Ⓑ Ⓒ Ⓓ   34. Ⓐ Ⓑ Ⓒ Ⓓ   44. Ⓐ Ⓑ Ⓒ Ⓓ

5. Ⓐ Ⓑ Ⓒ Ⓓ   15. Ⓐ Ⓑ Ⓒ Ⓓ   25. Ⓐ Ⓑ Ⓒ Ⓓ   35. Ⓐ Ⓑ Ⓒ Ⓓ   45. Ⓐ Ⓑ Ⓒ Ⓓ

6. Ⓐ Ⓑ Ⓒ Ⓓ   16. Ⓐ Ⓑ Ⓒ Ⓓ   26. Ⓐ Ⓑ Ⓒ Ⓓ   36. Ⓐ Ⓑ Ⓒ Ⓓ

7. Ⓐ Ⓑ Ⓒ Ⓓ   17. Ⓐ Ⓑ Ⓒ Ⓓ   27. Ⓐ Ⓑ Ⓒ Ⓓ   37. Ⓐ Ⓑ Ⓒ Ⓓ

8. Ⓐ Ⓑ Ⓒ Ⓓ   18. Ⓐ Ⓑ Ⓒ Ⓓ   28. Ⓐ Ⓑ Ⓒ Ⓓ   38. Ⓐ Ⓑ Ⓒ Ⓓ

9. Ⓐ Ⓑ Ⓒ Ⓓ   19. Ⓐ Ⓑ Ⓒ Ⓓ   29. Ⓐ Ⓑ Ⓒ Ⓓ   39. Ⓐ Ⓑ Ⓒ Ⓓ

10. Ⓐ Ⓑ Ⓒ Ⓓ   20. Ⓐ Ⓑ Ⓒ Ⓓ   30. Ⓐ Ⓑ Ⓒ Ⓓ   40. Ⓐ Ⓑ Ⓒ Ⓓ

answer sheet

Practice Test 2

45 Questions • 35 Minutes

Directions: In questions 1–45, each sentence has a word or phrase underlined. Below each sentence are four other words or phrases, marked **(A)**, **(B)**, **(C)**, and **(D)**. You are to choose the *one* word or phrase that *best keeps the meaning* of the original sentence if it is substituted for the underlined word or phrase. Then, on your answer sheet, find the number of the question and blacken the space that corresponds to the letter you have chosen so that the letter inside the oval cannot be seen.

Q The American Revolution was fought to gain <u>autonomy</u>.
- **(A)** self-righteousness
- **(B)** self-satisfaction
- **(C)** self-rule
- **(D)** self-reformation

A **The correct answer is (C),** *self-rule*. The Revolution, as you may already know, was the War of Independence, which is the same as *self-rule*.

1. He had reached the <u>zenith</u> of his career when he became president of General Motors.
   - **(A)** ambition
   - **(B)** zeal
   - **(C)** moment
   - **(D)** summit

2. The road west gave <u>access</u> to the lake.
   - **(A)** ascendancy
   - **(B)** approach
   - **(C)** protection
   - **(D)** asset

3. Because Jack <u>defaulted</u> on his loan, the bank took him to court.
   - **(A)** defamed his character
   - **(B)** erred in judgment
   - **(C)** paid in full
   - **(D)** failed to pay

4. Today's chemists seek a <u>panacea</u> for the world's ills.
   - **(A)** gold
   - **(B)** chemical
   - **(C)** release
   - **(D)** remedy

5. After years of <u>litigation</u>, the will was settled.
   - **(A)** illness
   - **(B)** lawsuits
   - **(C)** longevity
   - **(D)** taxes

6. Boutiques cater to a young <u>clientele</u>.
   - **(A)** dress style
   - **(B)** customers
   - **(C)** adolescent
   - **(D)** class

7. The styles that are in <u>vogue</u> in Paris change every year.

   (A) repute

   (B) length

   (C) fashion

   (D) brevity

8. The builder's <u>conservative</u> estimate of the time required to remodel the kitchen was six weeks.

   (A) reactionary

   (B) cautious

   (C) protective

   (D) traditional

9. Christian's path was <u>beset</u> by peril.

   (A) surrounded

   (B) chased

   (C) frightened

   (D) bested

10. The <u>precedent</u> for this case was set by a law passed in 1900.

    (A) precept

    (B) example

    (C) jurisdiction

    (D) pace

11. Frequent minor <u>ailments</u> kept her home from work.

    (A) irritations

    (B) young children

    (C) sicknesses

    (D) falls

12. The neighbors' constant <u>wrangles</u> with each other shattered our tranquility.

    (A) wrecks

    (B) wraths

    (C) quarrels

    (D) conversations

13. The Red Cross made an <u>equitable</u> distribution of the meals to the starving children.

    (A) just

    (B) quick

    (C) nutritious

    (D) convenient

14. When you apply for a loan, you must show that you have <u>assets</u> to cover the amount of the loan.

    (A) assessments

    (B) items of value

    (C) legal documents

    (D) stocks

15. The union members <u>boycotted</u> the meeting because they did not want to go on strike.

    (A) attended

    (B) blackmailed

    (C) shunned

    (D) left

16. The Industrial Revolution marked the beginning of an <u>epoch</u> of exodus from rural areas to cities.

    (A) episode

    (B) period

    (C) migration

    (D) story

17. <u>Participants</u> from 100 countries go to the Olympic Games.

    (A) people who buy things

    (B) people who watch

    (C) people who take part

    (D) people who travel

18. He got a gold medal for the <u>feat</u> of lifting 500 pounds.

    (A) accomplishment

    (B) fear

    (C) trial

    (D) event

19. We had to list the <u>chronology</u> of events in World War II on our test.

    (A) catastrophe

    (B) time sequence

    (C) disaster

    (D) discrepancy

20. You may find that jogging is <u>detrimental</u> rather than beneficial to your health.

    (A) helpful

    (B) facile

    (C) depressing

    (D) harmful

21. The power failure at 7 a.m. caused <u>consternation</u> among the city's commuters.

    (A) disability

    (B) deliberation

    (C) dismay

    (D) distaste

22. The hostess was <u>affronted</u> by Bill's failure to thank her for dinner.

    (A) affable

    (B) insulted

    (C) afflicted

    (D) confronted

23. His drunken behavior at the wedding was <u>deplorable</u>.

    (A) intoxicated

    (B) displayed

    (C) delightful

    (D) wretched

24. The <u>tainted</u> meat made him desperately ill.

    (A) contaminated

    (B) touched

    (C) refrigerated

    (D) colored

25. The <u>consensus</u> among the senators was that the bill would not be passed.

    (A) controversy

    (B) gathering

    (C) divided

    (D) agreement

26. I can jog a few miles, but the Boston Marathon is certainly beyond my <u>scope</u>.

    (A) view

    (B) opportunity

    (C) range

    (D) score

27. <u>Militant</u> suffragettes demanded the right to vote.

    (A) feminine

    (B) strongly committed

    (C) organized

    (D) newly liberated

28. <u>Currently</u>, there are at least four movies playing that deserve the Academy Award.

    (A) downtown

    (B) at the present time

    (C) at the local theater

    (D) frequently

29. The embarrassed young mother <u>admonished</u> her children for having taken the candy from the grocery shelf.

    (A) worried

    (B) reminded

    (C) scolded

    (D) praised

30. The dental work made a <u>profound</u> change in her appearance.

    (A) thorough

    (B) provocative

    (C) proper

    (D) interesting

31. The Browns were in a <u>dilemma</u> about whether to buy a house in the country or an apartment in the city where they worked.

    (A) predicament

    (B) discussion

    (C) agreement

    (D) stage

32. <u>Tempestuous</u> times preceded the declaration of war.

    (A) peaceful

    (B) emotionally charged

    (C) trying

    (D) temperate

33. Citizens who <u>collaborated</u> with the enemy during the war were executed after the war.

    (A) resisted

    (B) fought

    (C) lost

    (D) helped

34. A <u>versatile</u> material for home construction is wood.

    (A) useful

    (B) various

    (C) inflammable

    (D) common

35. Current laws protect <u>wildlife</u> from useless slaughter.

    (A) undomesticated animals

    (B) birds

    (C) nature

    (D) predators

36. Her refusal to go out with him <u>infuriated</u> him.

    (A) saddened

    (B) intoxicated

    (C) angered

    (D) frightened

37. Participation in <u>intramural</u> sports is required.

    (A) within the school

    (B) with outsiders

    (C) overly strenuous

    (D) extraordinary

38. On the <u>brink</u> of matrimony, he fled to a desert island.

    (A) ship

    (B) proposal

    (C) edge

    (D) evasion

39. The professor <u>elicited</u> a loud groan from his students with his difficult assignment.

    (A) eluded

    (B) repeated

    (C) drew out

    (D) articulated

40. City dwellers are <u>exhilarated</u> by the brisk country air.

    (A) amazed

    (B) fanned

    (C) humbled

    (D) stimulated

41. Ponce de Leon searched for magic waters to <u>rejuvenate</u> the elderly.

    (A) make young again

    (B) clean again

    (C) reject again

    (D) stimulate again

42. Although they had never met before the party, Roger and Gina felt a strong <u>affinity</u> to each other at first glance.

    (A) affability

    (B) attraction

    (C) dislike

    (D) interest

43. A person who suffers from stage fright is easily <u>intimidated</u> by a large audience.

(A) inspired

(B) applauded

(C) frightened

(D) expelled

44. Every other woman at the premiere was aware of the star's <u>ostentatious</u> display of her emeralds.

(A) wealthy

(B) loud

(C) oscillating

(D) showy

45. Young people often <u>dispense with</u> the traditional ceremonies of marriage.

(A) engage upon

(B) unite

(C) destroy

(D) omit

ANSWER KEY AND EXPLANATIONS

1.	D	10.	B	19.	B	28.	B	37.	A
2.	B	11.	C	20.	D	29.	C	38.	C
3.	D	12.	C	21.	C	30.	A	39.	C
4.	D	13.	A	22.	B	31.	A	40.	D
5.	B	14.	B	23.	D	32.	B	41.	A
6.	B	15.	C	24.	A	33.	D	42.	B
7.	C	16.	B	25.	D	34.	A	43.	C
8.	B	17.	C	26.	C	35.	A	44.	D
9.	A	18.	A	27.	B	36.	C	45.	D

1. **The correct answer is (D).** The *summit* is the highest point and, in this sentence, the presidency of the company can be viewed as the top position. The other answer choices do not make a meaningful sentence.

2. **The correct answer is (B).** Access is a way or means of reaching or entering a place. *Ascendancy* means domination and an *asset* is an advantage or important thing. *Protection* makes no sense in this sentence.

3. **The correct answer is (D).** *Defamed his character* and *erred in judgment* do not make a meaningful sentence. If you know that *paid in full* and *failed to pay* have opposite meaning, then you can assume that one of them is the correct answer. If Jack had *paid in full*, then the bank would not be inclined to take him to court.

4. **The correct answer is (D).** A panacea is something that is believed to cure all ills and problems. *Gold, chemical,* and *release* do not make sense in the sentence.

5. **The correct answer is (B).** *Litigation* is a lawsuit. The other answer choices do not make a meaningful sentence.

6. **The correct answer is (B).** The key word in the sentence is *cater*. To cater to someone is to satisfy his or her special needs. In this sentence, the special needs are of the young *customers*.

7. **The correct answer is (C).** *Vogue* usually refers to fashion.

8. **The correct answer is (B).** *Reactionary, protective,* or *traditional* would not describe the experience of obtaining an estimate of cost.

9. **The correct answer is (A).** *Beset* is to come at a target from all directions. The other answer choices do not make a meaningful sentence.

10. **The correct answer is (B).** This is a more difficult word because *precept* and *example* could be used to make a meaningful sentence. If you do not know the meaning of the words given as alternatives, add them to your card list.

11. **The correct answer is (C).** Although *irritations, young children,* and *falls* may keep someone home from work, *ailments* are sicknesses.

12. **The correct answer is (C).** The key word in the sentence is *shattered*, which means "to ruin or destroy."

13. **The correct answer is (A).** While the distribution of the meals might have been *quick, nutritious,* and perhaps, *convenient*, no one could dispute that the distribution was dictated by reason, conscience, and a natural sense of fairness.

14. **The correct answer is (B).** *Assets* are items of value to a person, business, or institution.

15. **The correct answer is (C).** A *boycott* is a refusal for political reasons to buy certain products or do business with a certain store or company. Although *left* would make a meaningful sentence, to boycott the meeting would be a refusal to attend.

16. **The correct answer is (B).** An *epoch* is a particular period of history. In this sentence, the epoch refers to the period during the Industrial Revolution when people moved from the country to the cities.

17. **The correct answer is (C).** A *participant* is someone who takes part in something.

18. **The correct answer is (A).** A *feat* is an act of skill, endurance, or strength. It is also an achievement. In this sentence, the gold medal was awarded for the achievement of lifting 500 pounds.

19. **The correct answer is (B).** A *chronology* is the arrangement of events in order of occurrence.

20. **The correct answer is (D).** *Beneficial* and *detrimental* are opposites.

21. **The correct answer is (C).** *Consternation* is surprise, confusion, and often anger directed toward an event or person.

22. **The correct answer is (B).** The key word is *failure*. None of the other answer choices makes sense in the sentence.

23. **The correct answer is (D).** His drunken behavior was considered "very bad."

24. **The correct answer is (A).** *Tainted* food is spoiled or contaminated.

25. **The correct answer is (D).** A *consensus* is an agreement reached among members of a group.

26. **The correct answer is (C).** *Scope* represents the limits or range of something.

27. **The correct answer is (B).** *Militants* are strongly committed to a cause.

28. **The correct answer is (B).**

29. **The correct answer is (C).** *Admonished* means to criticize or scold. The key word in the sentence is *embarrassed*. None of the other answer choices makes sense in the sentence.

30. **The correct answer is (A).**

31. **The correct answer is (A).** A *dilemma* usually refers to a situation in which a choice *must* be made.

32. **The correct answer is (B).**

33. **The correct answer is (D).** The prefix *co-* means "with."

34. **The correct answer is (A).** *Versatile* means useful in many ways or multipurpose.

35. **The correct answer is (A).**

36. **The correct answer is (C).**

37. **The correct answer is (A).** The prefix "intra-" means *within*. *Intramural* means within an organization.

38. **The correct answer is (C).** *Brink* can mean the top edge of a cliff or, in this sentence, a point after which something may happen.

39. **The correct answer is (C).** *Elicit* means to get or to bring out.

40. **The correct answer is (D).** People often refer to brisk air as *exhilarating* since it makes them feel strong and happy.

41. **The correct answer is (A).** The Latin root is "iuvenis," young. *Rejuvenate* is to make young again.

42. **The correct answer is (B).** The couple felt an attraction to each other. *Affability* is easy to talk to.

43. **The correct answer is (C).** To *intimidate* is to make someone fearful. The key word in the sentence is *suffers*.

44. **The correct answer is (D).** *Ostentatious* displays are intended to attract some notice and to impress other people.

45. **The correct answer is (D).** To *dispense with* means to manage without or to get rid of.

ANSWER SHEET PRACTICE TEST 3

1. Ⓐ Ⓑ Ⓒ Ⓓ   11. Ⓐ Ⓑ Ⓒ Ⓓ   21. Ⓐ Ⓑ Ⓒ Ⓓ   31. Ⓐ Ⓑ Ⓒ Ⓓ   41. Ⓐ Ⓑ Ⓒ Ⓓ

2. Ⓐ Ⓑ Ⓒ Ⓓ   12. Ⓐ Ⓑ Ⓒ Ⓓ   22. Ⓐ Ⓑ Ⓒ Ⓓ   32. Ⓐ Ⓑ Ⓒ Ⓓ   42. Ⓐ Ⓑ Ⓒ Ⓓ

3. Ⓐ Ⓑ Ⓒ Ⓓ   13. Ⓐ Ⓑ Ⓒ Ⓓ   23. Ⓐ Ⓑ Ⓒ Ⓓ   33. Ⓐ Ⓑ Ⓒ Ⓓ   43. Ⓐ Ⓑ Ⓒ Ⓓ

4. Ⓐ Ⓑ Ⓒ Ⓓ   14. Ⓐ Ⓑ Ⓒ Ⓓ   24. Ⓐ Ⓑ Ⓒ Ⓓ   34. Ⓐ Ⓑ Ⓒ Ⓓ   44. Ⓐ Ⓑ Ⓒ Ⓓ

5. Ⓐ Ⓑ Ⓒ Ⓓ   15. Ⓐ Ⓑ Ⓒ Ⓓ   25. Ⓐ Ⓑ Ⓒ Ⓓ   35. Ⓐ Ⓑ Ⓒ Ⓓ   45. Ⓐ Ⓑ Ⓒ Ⓓ

6. Ⓐ Ⓑ Ⓒ Ⓓ   16. Ⓐ Ⓑ Ⓒ Ⓓ   26. Ⓐ Ⓑ Ⓒ Ⓓ   36. Ⓐ Ⓑ Ⓒ Ⓓ

7. Ⓐ Ⓑ Ⓒ Ⓓ   17. Ⓐ Ⓑ Ⓒ Ⓓ   27. Ⓐ Ⓑ Ⓒ Ⓓ   37. Ⓐ Ⓑ Ⓒ Ⓓ

8. Ⓐ Ⓑ Ⓒ Ⓓ   18. Ⓐ Ⓑ Ⓒ Ⓓ   28. Ⓐ Ⓑ Ⓒ Ⓓ   38. Ⓐ Ⓑ Ⓒ Ⓓ

9. Ⓐ Ⓑ Ⓒ Ⓓ   19. Ⓐ Ⓑ Ⓒ Ⓓ   29. Ⓐ Ⓑ Ⓒ Ⓓ   39. Ⓐ Ⓑ Ⓒ Ⓓ

10. Ⓐ Ⓑ Ⓒ Ⓓ   20. Ⓐ Ⓑ Ⓒ Ⓓ   30. Ⓐ Ⓑ Ⓒ Ⓓ   40. Ⓐ Ⓑ Ⓒ Ⓓ

answer sheet

Practice Test 3

45 Questions • 35 Minutes

Directions: In questions 1–45 each sentence has a word or phrase underlined. Below each sentence are four other words or phrases, marked **(A), (B), (C),** and **(D).** You are to choose the *one* word or phrase that *best keeps the meaning* of the original sentence if it is substituted for the underlined word or phrase. Then, on your answer sheet, find the number of the question and blacken the space that corresponds to the letter you have chosen so that the letter inside the oval cannot be seen.

Q He talked so fast that I couldn't <u>comprehend</u> what he said.

(A) hear

(B) translate

(C) understand

(D) repeat

A **The correct answer is (C),** *understand*, because logically you would not understand fast speech. You could *hear* him. No mention is made of his speaking in a foreign language, so *translate* is not a likely answer. *Repeat* is out of the question in this context.

1. Some believe that the treatment for alcoholism is complete <u>abstinence</u> from alcohol.

(A) absence

(B) avoidance

(C) sickness

(D) prescription

2. Savage hordes swept across Europe and <u>ruthlessly</u> attacked all in their path.

(A) without stopping

(B) without weapons

(C) without warning

(D) without pity

3. Many of the <u>habitats</u> of birds and plants have been destroyed by man's pollution.

(A) nests

(B) forests

(C) natural homes

(D) grounds

4. Children have a <u>jargon</u> of their own that their elders frequently don't understand.

(A) unintelligible talk

(B) exercise plan

(C) strange gait

(D) sign language

5. The UN delegates lived in <u>temporary</u> housing until their apartment house was constructed.

(A) timely

(B) temperate

(C) limited time

(D) temporizing

6. Chinese <u>cuisine</u> specializes in rice dishes.

(A) delicacies

(B) cooking

(C) chefs

(D) gourmets

7. It was <u>inevitable</u> that women would be sent into space along with men.

(A) unlikely

(B) fantastic

(C) influential

(D) unavoidable

8. One of the <u>superstitions</u> related to weddings is that the bride should wear something blue.

(A) rules of conduct

(B) irrational beliefs

(C) nuptials

(D) religious ceremonies

9. The Industrial Revolution <u>effected</u> a drastic change in the British standard of living in the 18th century.

(A) caused

(B) eliminated

(C) prevented

(D) denied

10. The colonists made a <u>vehement</u> protest against taxation without representation.

(A) veiled

(B) verified

(C) impassioned

(D) voracious

11. Whenever I have to make a speech, the minute I stand up on the <u>dais</u> I forget every word.

(A) front

(B) feet

(C) soap box

(D) platform

12. Food manufacturers must <u>label</u> their products with content information.

(A) sell

(B) describe

(C) brand

(D) stick on

13. After camping in the wilderness for two weeks, he was so <u>unkempt</u> that his wife was horrified.

(A) extremely messy

(B) ugly

(C) totally ferocious

(D) undone

14. Two small toy manufacturers <u>consolidated</u> to form a new business.

(A) advertised

(B) united

(C) divided

(D) met

15. His wife's <u>extravagant</u> tastes put him in debt.

(A) excessive

(B) extraordinary

(C) exclusive

(D) exciting

16. After her husband's death, Mrs. Brown spent several <u>melancholy</u> years alone in her apartment.

(A) tired

(B) meaningful

(C) brief

(D) sad

17. Because he swam too fast at the beginning of the race, he lost his <u>stamina</u> early.

    (A) energy

    (B) place

    (C) stand

    (D) stroke

18. If you stay on this diet, <u>ultimately</u> you will lose weight.

    (A) formerly

    (B) finally

    (C) unlikely

    (D) possibly

19. He studied so <u>zealously</u> that he graduated from college first in his class.

    (A) lazily

    (B) enthusiastically

    (C) happily

    (D) dispassionately

20. His physical condition was no <u>impediment</u> to his career as a violinist.

    (A) help

    (B) impatience

    (C) hindrance

    (D) impossibility

21. You <u>ought to</u> read the directions carefully before you begin the problems.

    (A) may

    (B) might

    (C) should

    (D) can

22. An author in the <u>throes</u> of creation hates to be interrupted.

    (A) struggle

    (B) study

    (C) wake

    (D) theater

23. A diabetic has to <u>renounce</u> most sugar in his diet.

    (A) give up

    (B) foresee

    (C) inject

    (D) curse

24. Chicago became <u>notorious</u> for crime and corruption during the days of Prohibition.

    (A) disrupted

    (B) evil

    (C) known

    (D) criminal

25. The course of studies is <u>geared</u> to an urban population.

    (A) driven

    (B) modified

    (C) apparent

    (D) tried

26. Physical infirmity often makes people <u>querulous</u> and hard to live with.

    (A) irritable

    (B) weak

    (C) indignant

    (D) poor

27. The French restaurant in our neighborhood is a favorite <u>rendezvous</u> for parents without their children.

    (A) hidden retreat

    (B) hiding place

    (C) meeting place

    (D) dining room

28. The ship <u>foundered</u> on the rocks during the hurricane.

    (A) established

    (B) struck

    (C) failed

    (D) sank

29. The Salk vaccine has had a <u>potent</u> effect upon the incidence of polio.

(A) potential
(B) powerful
(C) praiseworthy
(D) priceless

30. At the age of ninety, her health has <u>regressed</u> to the point that she may soon die.

(A) remembered
(B) alluded
(C) deteriorated
(D) progressed

31. Americans were <u>appalled</u> by the latest statistics regarding violent crimes.

(A) mildly surprised
(B) informed
(C) shocked
(D) pleased

32. John blamed his poor grades this semester upon his having participated in too many <u>extracurricular</u> activities.

(A) frivolous and additional
(B) athletic and vigorous
(C) outside the curriculum
(D) inattentive to studies

33. <u>Furthermore</u>, I feel that his behavior is upsetting the entire classroom.

(A) Nevertheless
(B) However
(C) In spite of this
(D) In addition

34. I <u>infer</u> from our conversation that he has no intention of paying the bill.

(A) conclude
(B) intrude
(C) imply
(D) hear

35. <u>Toxic</u> waste from nuclear plants is hazardous to the environment.

(A) troublesome
(B) poisonous
(C) grievous
(D) panic

36. As she aged, she became so <u>garrulous</u> that no one else could be heard.

(A) talkative
(B) gracious
(C) sickly
(D) grey

37. Obviously Helen's <u>forte</u> is chemistry.

(A) fortitude
(B) talent
(C) weakness
(D) fixation

38. That the government ought to develop a jobs program seemed to Congress an <u>indisputable</u> fact.

(A) indefinite
(B) indispensable
(C) unquestionable
(D) undefinable

39. The electrician was <u>scrupulous</u> about grounding all the wires in the factory.

(A) afraid
(B) employed
(C) careful
(D) infamous

40. The <u>interment</u> took place last Friday.

(A) festivity
(B) installation
(C) launching
(D) burial

41. We all have <u>peccadillos</u> that our intimate friends tolerate.

    (A) small faults

    (B) bad habits

    (C) assigned duties

    (D) foul language

42. Her disapproval was <u>implicit</u> in her response to his behavior.

    (A) implicated

    (B) important

    (C) implied

    (D) impious

43. All of the President's efforts to <u>rescind</u> the law were unavailing.

    (A) revive

    (B) change

    (C) repeal

    (D) rescue

44. The Senator has a <u>vindictive</u> attitude toward her ex-husband.

    (A) vindicated

    (B) troublesome

    (C) weak

    (D) vengeful

45. In the <u>interim</u> between performances, the famous actress toured Europe.

    (A) interval

    (B) interception

    (C) interaction

    (D) insertion

ANSWER KEY AND EXPLANATIONS

1.	B	10.	C	19.	B	28.	D	37. B
2.	D	11.	D	20.	C	29.	B	38. C
3.	C	12.	B	21.	C	30.	C	39. C
4.	A	13.	A	22.	A	31.	C	40. D
5.	C	14.	B	23.	A	32.	C	41. A
6.	B	15.	A	24.	C	33.	D	42. C
7.	D	16.	D	25.	B	34.	A	43. C
8.	B	17.	A	26.	A	35.	B	44. D
9.	A	18.	B	27.	C	36.	A	45. A

1. **The correct answer is (B).** *Abstinence* is usually used to describe the avoidance of alcohol.

2. **The correct answer is (D).** *Ruthlessly* is having no compassion or pity. A synonym for *ruthless* is merciless.

3. **The correct answer is (C).** *Habitat* refers to the environment where an organism, animal, or plant normally lives or occurs. Although birds live in *nests* and *forests* contain plants, (C) best keeps the meaning of the original sentence if it is substituted for *habitats*.

4. **The correct answer is (A).** *Jargon* can refer either to a specialized or technical language or nonsensical talk. The other answer choices do not make a meaningful sentence when substituted for *jargon*.

5. **The correct answer is (C).** The Latin prefix, tempor-, refers to time. *Timely* refers to something occurring at a suitable time but does not make a meaningful sentence when substituted for *temporary*.

6. **The correct answer is (B).** *Cuisine* is the manner of preparing food.

7. **The correct answer is (D).** An *inevitable* event or occurrence is an *unavoidable* event or occurrence.

8. **The correct answer is (B).** *Superstitions* are irrational beliefs that are sometimes rooted in magic or the supernatural.

9. **The correct answer is (A).** An *effect* is a result; the verb, effect, means to produce a result.

10. **The correct answer is (C).** The other answer choices do not make a meaningful sentence.

11. **The correct answer is (D).** A *dais* is a platform usually with chairs, a long table, and a podium for speakers at a banquet or a lecture.

12. **The correct answer is (B).** The noun, *label*, is a marker on a product that is used to give its name and contents. Here, the verb, *label*, is to mark with a label.

13. **The correct answer is (A).** The key word in the sentence is *horrified*. It is obvious by the wife's response that the man looked unlike himself.

14. **The correct answer is (B).** The prefix con- means "with." To *consolidate* is to group together to reduce in number.

15. **The correct answer is (A).**

16. **The correct answer is (D).**

17. **The correct answer is (A).** *Stamina* is the ability to exercise or work for long periods of time.

18. **The correct answer is (B).**

19. **The correct answer is (B).**

20. **The correct answer is (C).** An *impediment* is something that prevents or interferes with something.

21. **The correct answer is (C).** *Ought* is used to express an obligation.

22. **The correct answer is (A).** It is a condition of agonizing struggle.

23. **The correct answer is (A).** A person with diabetes should limit his or her intake of sugar.

24. **The correct answer is (C).** *Notorious* is well-known or famous, especially for something bad.

25. **The correct answer is (B).** The phrase, "to *gear* something to," is to make something suitable.

26. **The correct answer is (A).** A *querulous* person finds something wrong with everything.

27. **The correct answer is (C).** A *rendezvous* is a meeting place. The word is also used to describe a meeting, especially between lovers.

28. **The correct answer is (D).** To *founder* can mean to trip or fall from great tiredness, but, in this sentence, *foundered* is to fill up with water and sink.

29. **The correct answer is (B).** A *potent* drug has a strong effect or influence, making it very powerful. The other answer choices do not make a meaningful sentence.

30. **The correct answer is (C).** To *regress* is to go backwards, usually to a worse condition.

31. **The correct answer is (C).** The other answer choices make little sense, given the subject matter of the sentence.

32. **The correct answer is (C).** The prefix *extra-* means "out of."

33. **The correct answer is (D).** A synonym would be "moreover."

34. **The correct answer is (A).** To *infer* is to come to a conclusion based on some information.

35. **The correct answer is (B).** The other answer choices do not make a meaningful sentence.

36. **The correct answer is (A).** A *garrulous* person talks too much.

37. **The correct answer is (B).** A *forte* is something that a person does well.

38. **The correct answer is (C).**

39. **The correct answer is (C).** A *scrupulous* person is attentive to detail and correctness.

40. **The correct answer is (D).** To *inter* is to bury.

41. **The correct answer is (A).** This is from the Spanish "peccadillo."

42. **The correct answer is (C).** An *implicit* agreement is one that is implied or understood, without being directly expressed.

43. **The correct answer is (C).**

44. **The correct answer is (D).** A *vindictive* person seeks to harm another person.

45. **The correct answer is (A).** An *interim* is a time period between events.

answers practice test 3

NOTES

NOTES

NOTES

NOTES

NOTES

NOTES

NOTES

DATE DUE

Peterson's
Book Satisfaction Survey

Give Us Your Feedback

Thank you for choosing Peterson's as your source for personalized solutions for your education and career achievement. Please take a few minutes to answer the following questions. Your answers will go a long way in helping us to produce the most user-friendly and comprehensive resources to meet your individual needs.

When completed, please tear out this page and mail it to us at:

Publishing Department
PETERSON'S, A Nelnet Company
2000 Lenox Drive
Lawrenceville, NJ 08648

You can also complete this survey online at **www.petersons.com/booksurvey.**

1. **What is the ISBN of the book you have purchased? (The ISBN can be found on the book's back cover in the lower right-hand corner.)** _____

2. **Where did you purchase this book?**
   ❑ Retailer, such as Barnes & Noble
   ❑ Online reseller, such as Amazon.com
   ❑ Petersons.com
   ❑ Other (please specify) _____

3. **If you purchased this book on Petersons.com, please rate the following aspects of your online purchasing experience on a scale of 4 to 1 (4 = Excellent and 1 = Poor).**

	4	3	2	1
Comprehensiveness of Peterson's Online Bookstore page	❑	❑	❑	❑
Overall online customer experience	❑	❑	❑	❑

4. **Which category best describes you?**
   ❑ High school student
   ❑ Parent of high school student
   ❑ College student
   ❑ Graduate/professional student
   ❑ Returning adult student
   ❑ Teacher
   ❑ Counselor
   ❑ Working professional/military
   ❑ Other (please specify) _____

5. **Rate your overall satisfaction with this book.**

Extremely Satisfied	Satisfied	Not Satisfied
❑	❑	❑

6. **Rate each of the following aspects of this book on a scale of 4 to 1 (4 = Excellent and 1 = Poor).**

	4	3	2	1
Comprehensiveness of the information	❑	❑	❑	❑
Accuracy of the information	❑	❑	❑	❑
Usability	❑	❑	❑	❑
Cover design	❑	❑	❑	❑
Book layout	❑	❑	❑	❑
Special features (e.g., CD, flashcards, charts, etc.)	❑	❑	❑	❑
Value for the money	❑	❑	❑	❑

7. **This book was recommended by:**
   - ❑ Guidance counselor
   - ❑ Parent/guardian
   - ❑ Family member/relative
   - ❑ Friend
   - ❑ Teacher
   - ❑ Not recommended by anyone—I found the book on my own
   - ❑ Other (please specify) _____

8. **Would you recommend this book to others?**

Yes	Not Sure	No
❑	❑	❑

9. **Please provide any additional comments.**

_____

_____

_____

_____

_____

Remember, you can tear out this page and mail it to us at:

Publishing Department
PETERSON'S, A Nelnet Company
2000 Lenox Drive
Lawrenceville, NJ 08648

or you can complete the survey online at **www.petersons.com/booksurvey.**

Your feedback is important to us at Peterson's, and we thank you for your time!

If you would like us to keep in touch with you about new products and services, please include your e-mail here: _____